I Reserve the Right
to Be Terrified

~

A LONG LIFE

I Reserve the Right to Be Terrified

A LONG LIFE

~

Blayney Colmore

GREEN PLACE BOOKS | *Brattleboro, Vermont*

Copyright © 2022 by Blayney Colmore.

All rights reserved. No part of this book may be reproduced in
any manner without written permission except in the case of brief
quotations included in critical articles and reviews.

Printed in the United States

10 9 8 7 6 5 4 3 2 1

GREEN WRITERS PRESS is a Vermont-based publisher whose mission
is to spread a message of hope and renewal through the words and
images we publish. Throughout we will adhere to our commitment to
preserving and protecting the natural resources of the earth. To that
end, a percentage of our proceeds will be donated to environmental,
and social-justice activist groups. Green Writers Press gratefully
acknowledges support from individual donors, friends, and readers to
help support the environment and our publishing initiative. GREEN
PLACE BOOKS curates books that tell literary and compelling stories
with a focus on writing about place.

GREEN
PLACE
BOOKS

GReen
wriTers
press

Giving Voice to Writers & Artists Who Will Make the World a Better Place

Green Writers Press | Brattleboro, Vermont
www.greenwriterspress.com

ISBN: 979-8-9865324-8-6

Cover photo used with permission of John Thiele.

THE PAPER USED IN THIS PUBLICATION IS PRODUCED BY MILLS COMMITTED
TO RESPONSIBLE AND SUSTAINABLE FORESTRY PRACTICES.

The older I get, the more clearly I remember things
that never happened.

—MARK TWAIN

~

After you die your hair and fingernails continue to grow,
but the phone calls taper off.

—JOHNNY CARSON

The Big Downhill

The road was steep. But it leveled off at the bottom, so you got a nice glide before the next hill. We'd ridden that road a lot, so we let the bikes run. Last I looked at the speedometer it read between 30 and 35 miles per hour.

Exhilarating.

Conrad and his daughter Karen were much more experienced and stronger bikers than I was. I followed them down the hill. They both skillfully avoided the board in the road. I never saw it.

He told me later that he saw me launch from my bike like a rocket. "You must have gone 20 feet in the air before you landed." When Karen saw me lying motionless on the road, she said, "Oh God, Dad, I think he's dead."

Conrad went into a nearby house to call an ambulance, and Lacey, my wife "The good news," he said to Lacey, "looks like he's regained consciousness."

Though nothing was broken, I had suffered a concussion and scraped several layers of skin off my back and face.

I don't remember much of the ambulance ride to Brattleboro Hospital. In our small village of Jacksonville, Vermont, the paramedics are neighbors. The woman tending to me in the back of the ambulance tried to engage me in conversation. I must have talked some because the driver said, "Sounds like he's OK."

"I know this guy," the woman by my side said, "He's *not* OK."

That wasn't the first time I understood how fragile our hold on this life is. Ever since my dog was killed by a car when I was 8, I've wondered what it must be like to die.

Though I made a full recovery (the dermatologist looks at the scars on my back and asks, "What the hell happened to you?"), my sense of how suddenly we can lose that hold was deepened.

I think about death a lot. I always have.

Don't you?

A Drop of Water

Maybe the best description for what I make of death is ambivalence.

I asked my therapist if he ever finds himself looking forward to dying as relief from the stresses of living. "Oh yes," he said, "but until then I reserve the right to be terrified."

Knowing more certainly with each passing day that I will die, sooner than later, I have written in tiny hand-writing on some of my journal pages:

Life's a bitch
You're not important
Your life is not about you
You're going to die

In larger handwriting:
Who are you
Who am I
O God Make Speed to Save Us

O Lord Make Haste to Help Us
Praise Ye The Lord
The Lord's Name be Praised

We can't know God
We can only love God
Or anyone
Everyone
Apophatic
Knowing by silence and symbol

Midnight Mass

FROM NETFLIX SERIES

Riley: When we die. What happens?

Erin: Yeah, what the fuck happens.

Riley: So what do you think happens when we die, Erin?

Erin: Speaking for myself?

Riley: Speaking for yourself.

Erin: Myself. My self. That's the problem. That's the problem with the whole thing. That word, "self." That's not the word. That's not right. That isn't . . . That isn't. How did I forget that? When did I forget that?

The body stops one cell at a time, but the brain keeps firing those neurons. Like lightning bolts, like fireworks inside, and I thought I'd despair or feel afraid, but I don't feel any of that. None of it. Because I'm too busy. I'm too busy at this moment. Remembering. Of course. I remember that every atom in my body was forged in a star. This matter, this body, is mostly just empty space after all, and solid matter? It's just energy vibrating very slowly and there is no me. There never was. The electrons of my body mingle and dance with the electrons of the ground below me and the air I'm no longer breathing . . .

Just by remembering, we return home. Like a drop of water falling back into the ocean.

Garrett, My Life – Donor

A rogue hurricane in 1938 is the reason I'm here. My mother was on Fire Island. They had no idea what hurricanes were about. As the storm grew increasingly threatening, they evacuated their houses, went to the highest house, still only a few feet above sea level. Nerve-wracking. My mother, eight months pregnant, caught a terrible cold, with a hacking cough. She ended up giving premature birth to a boy who survived only minutes.

His name was to be Garrett.

Not long after, she became pregnant again. That turned out to be me. I doubt she would have conceived so soon again had the little boy lived. In some weird, palpable sense, Garrett gave his life to me.

•

Memories. Each of us, reassembled star dust. Memories, filtered through aging neurons, star dust, scattered, reassembled. For a season.

What Tribe?

Born in New Jersey, a place that now seems foreign, maybe even alien. Then we moved to North Carolina when I was 4, with 3-years-older, and 2-years-younger, sisters. Despite the shame, I can conjure about being formed in the post-war, segregated south, the place can still arouse warm feelings though I haven't lived there since we moved to The Philippines when I was 13. My roots remain tinged with the seemingly serene (for middle class Whites), 1950s segregated south.

One day walking home from a friend's house in Manila, I was suddenly surrounded by several Filipino boys about my age who had come out of a barrio near our house.

"Hey, white monkey," one of them challenged, "want to fight?"

"No," I said, knowing my fear was easy for them to see.

"For sport only," one boy said, as he unsheathed a Balisong, the Filipino equivalent of a switch blade.

My heart racing, adrenaline flowing, I sprinted in the direction of our house. The Filipino boys laughed, shouting, "White Monkey!" and making squawking sounds like a chicken.

It was my first experience of being on the other side of racial discrimination. Being called a white monkey made me aware of my different appearance being off-putting to some.

PTSD ?

There's a moment in Manila I often forget, which makes me wonder why. I was 11. Took a swim at the Polo Club. As I got out of the shower the assistant club manager walked by. He stopped, said something, then took my penis between his two fingers and said, "You're getting to be a big boy, aren't you?" I was uncomfortable but he was my elder so I endured it. That night I told Dad about it. I don't remember his making a big fuss. He asked me a few questions. I think he told me the manager shouldn't have done that. I don't know how long after that I realized that the manager wasn't at the club any more. I think I understood why, and remember feeling badly that I cost him his job. It didn't seem like he'd done such a terrible thing. All we read now about early sexual trauma makes me wonder if it left some mark on my psyche. I don't think I've ever become totally comfortable with sexual intimacy. Until the recent writing about early sexual abuse, it wouldn't have occurred to me to locate my discomfort in that moment.

Not sure I would now.

My natural shyness and lack of confidence with women seems more rooted in my personality than in trauma. But it has served to accentuate my sense of never quite being part of the cool cohort. Never part of locker room bragging about sexual conquests.

The sexual and drug experimenting soon to gain attention when I was the age of those who would be immersed in them were not quite yet fully cooked, still on the horizon. More of my friends than I realized were enjoying sex, and a few of the more daring were into marijuana. Life has always seemed too fragile to me to assume more risk than we face in the ordinary course of events. No doubt that left me out of a lot of the excitement, but something about making my way through every day provided enough unscheduled excitement for me.

Exiled at 14

Like most ex-pats, I was sent to boys boarding school in New England at 14. Then college in Philadelphia, three years of seminary in Cambridge, Massachusetts. After ordination, parishes in Akron, Ohio, Washington, D.C., Dedham, Massachusetts, La Jolla, California. Though each station provided rich experience, none settled the question of which tribe I belong to.

When people ask where I'm from I used to dial up that long list of places. One day a woman stopped me in mid-response.

"Where did you live when you were six and started school?" she asked.

"Charlotte," I said.

"Then that's where you're from."

Though I have little conscious identification with Charlotte, I get that. I lived there from 4 years old until 7th grade. A lot got lodged in me.

It seems clear that much of what forms us is below consciousness. I know much of what I learned from those years lies deeper in my bones than I can retrieve.

Bumpy Start

I was a poor student from the start. Likely dyslexic.

Miserable in boarding school where it began to feel like performance mattered. New England climate colder than I had ever experienced. The other boys and faculty even colder. No doubt my being young, 13,000 miles from home, before cell phones, contributed to my misery.

The first two years were spent at Kent, an Episcopal school modeled after English public schools. The senior boys ran everything except instruction. Nothing triggers more *Lord of the Flies* sadism than 17-year-old boys with authority over younger boys. The chapel worship was austere, formal, elaborate—what we once called High-Church. As alienating to me as all the rest of the school's life.

After failing just about everything (did I really flunk Sacred Studies?), I went to St. George's in Newport, Rhode Island, another, smaller, less formal Episcopal

School where faculty was fully engaged. Bill Schenck, a history teacher, took a liking to me. He was the first to wake my still largely dormant intellect, just as I was beginning to be curious about everything. I credit Bill with having rescued me from whatever disaster my life seemed headed for when I showed up at St. George's feeling defeated. He remained a friend until his death.

Was I aware then that no place felt like home? Sometimes, when I listened to people talk about their deep roots someplace, I could feel lost

Leaving family for distant schooling meant being effectively severed, permanently. Painfully.

One Christmas vacation my sister, Sylvia, and I were visiting grandparents in Charlotte. We made a reservation to phone our parents and younger sister, Perry, in Manila. A radio connection. After a two-day wait the call came through. Disaster.

The weak signal wouldn't carry female voices intelligibly. The conversation consisted of Dad and me—the two least good at making conversation—while Mom and my sisters sobbed.

Finally Home?

Fast forward more than 60 years.

Retired. Ready to try the writing I'd long wanted to do. We moved from a grand rectory in La Jolla, California, into our simple, 1830 farmhouse in rural, southern Vermont. We'd owned it since 1981, when we were living in Dedham. We'd take the occasional two-hour drive for a couple-of-days break. I'd never lived anywhere like rural, remote Jacksonville, Vermont. Nor in an old farmhouse.

Surprisingly, I have more sense of being home in that old farmhouse than I have anywhere before.

Curious, because the local people in the tiny, rural town will forever consider me a flatlander despite our having owned the place for over 40 years.

When I tell them where we live they say, "Oh, you live in Minnie Stetson's house." Our terrier and I walk across the road to the town burial ground and pause at

Minnie's grave. We give her an update on goings-on in her house. We've now lived there longer than Minnie did, but it remains Minnie's.

And ours.

Three years in seminary was being immersed in an alternate reality, richer than I'd ever experienced. I learned that ancient Hebrews consider us all sojourners, here for a season. Never fully at home anywhere.

One meaning of Hebrew, *Habiru*, is outsider, wanderer

My life, like ancient Hebrew lives, has wandered and strayed, chronically eager to belong, increasingly aware I never fully will. Anywhere.

We're a late-arriving species on this lush planet, perhaps just passing through. Almost every creature that this world has given birth to is no longer here.

Some mostly unacknowledged sense in us knows we won't be here forever. Not merely each of us, but our remarkable species.

We are a tribal species, eager to belong, but our tribal identity—maybe more than ever in the rootless, global 20th and 21st centuries—remains elusive.

You could argue that the fraught conflict we find ourselves in, more than two centuries after our founding as our country grows increasingly diverse, stems from our anxiety about who belongs. And about whether I belong. Is it possible for a nation made up mostly of immigrants from all over, to govern itself? Must my discomfort with being uncertain where, and if, I fit cause me to want to disenfranchise those different from me? Is it possible to find our differences as valuable and prized as our sameness?

No wonder our country is still considered an unproven experiment.

Loss

My first year in seminary a third-year student, soon to test his wings at higher altitude, preached a sermon at Evening Prayer in which he said, "Every relationship ends in loss."

I was startled, outraged. I'd absorbed the insight that Gospel preach translates as "Good News." That didn't sound like good news to me.

I figured the guy was showing off his 1960s Cambridge radicalism before he stepped into the big world where bishops and vestries sign preachers' paychecks.

Surely he didn't think he could preach that downer message to an Episcopalian congregation of mostly upward-struggling, middle-class managers.

Later that night over beer, we got talking about that sermon. When I said I'd been appalled, one of the others challenged me.

"That's simply logical reality," he said. "We're born, here for a while, then we die. It's only bad news if we're in denial about the reality of being transients, sojourners. Know anyone 200 years old?"

Nearly 60 years later that sermon remains vivid in memory. Now I understand it as another piece of our kinship with Zen insight encouraging us to sit loose in the saddle with our existence. We didn't initiate it, and we almost never decide when or how it will end.

What would it take for us to embrace our reality as wanderers? To love being here even though it's for a season?

It takes discipline.

Early in my time as rector of Dedham I invited Michael Dwinell to come preach. Michael had grown up in the parish, and he was now an ordained priest. He had given up on parish work, finding it frustrating to try to break through the entrenched habits and prejudices of upper middle-class Episcopalians. And he acknowledged his discomfort at seeing himself in so much of the world he grew up in and had worked so hard to overcome.

But he loved coming to preach to those he had known growing up, tweaking their comfort zone.

I had just gotten a Honda Civic, proud to have a shiny new car. I showed it off to Michael, pointing out the new features. Michael listened patiently. When I'd finished, he said, "Do you ever picture this car 10 years from now, flattened and rusting in a junkyard?"

No, I hadn't.

Now and Then

In 1966, twenty-six-years old, walking down the steps
of St. Paul's Cathedral, Boston, following the service
in which I was ordained, I found myself beside Henry
Knox Sherrill, who, if his name wasn't intimidating
enough, was an icon of the Episcopal Church. Bishop
of Massachusetts before being elevated to Presiding
Bishop of the United States, he was probably about the
age I am as I write this (82).

I managed to tame my awe just enough to ask after
his well-being. He paused, looked wistful.

"All I do now," he said, "is bury my friends."

Not sure at what age that student's sermon, and
Bishop Sherrill's soulful revelation evolved in my conscious from abstract to flesh-aging reality. It may have
been when I caught myself hoping I don't have to live
a lot longer, knowing as I age, I face accelerating losses.

That sense of impermanence has been etched a little deeper into all of us with the second, astonishingly

contagious Covid variant burning through our species as I write this in early 2022.

I'm something of a pariah to many, some in my own family, who find my chronic probing of what to make of loss and death no longer simply amusing eccentricity, but and unwelcome, often annoying reminder of what they'd rather not dwell on.

A few days before we moved from Dedham to La Jolla, we faced the reality that Lily, our 13-year-old terrier—blind, incontinent—couldn't make the move with us. I took her to the vet to be euthanized. Brought her slowly cooling body home where the kids had dug a hole for her. As we lowered her into the hole my grief overwhelmed me. I began sobbing. It alarmed the kids. It did me too. One of them asked Lacey if I would be all right. "I don't know," she admitted.

Recently a dear friend's widow asked me to give the homily at her husband's burial. I agonized over having to do that. As I preached, I lost my composure. In all the years, and in all the funeral homilies I preached, I don't think I ever lost my composure quite so totally.

I'm grateful for having regained the ability to cry in my old age, lost to me since early childhood. My body is becoming more willing to embrace grief and loss even though my busy intellect continues to want to fend it off.

Sobbing when someone I love dies, while unsettling, feels satisfying, essential to grieving. But I'll probably never break down, even in old age, without hearing the echo of my father's stern warning: "Stop crying

right now, or I'll give you something really worth crying about." He was within days of his death when he
broke down in tears saying goodbye to me. Whatever
embarrassment he would once have felt was erased by
his knowing he was dying. That helped leach some of
his old warning out of my bones.

For Better, For Worse

Marriage vows describe our connections to spouse, and, for that matter, to everyone who owns a piece of our psyche. Over a long lifetime that can include a lot of people. When we marry, we formally acknowledge those bonds as being for better and for worse, for richer and for poorer, in sickness and in health. Which of us is aware as we say those vows that we understand it means the bonds that connect us are so powerful they can't be severed, even when we wish they could be? The vows mean to have us admit that the ties, both blessing and burden, are not optional. If we can stay with it through the "For Worse" part it can become reassuring because, truth be told, what worries us most is not that we can't unload someone we're no longer enjoying being with, but that they might get sick of us and unload us.

The end of the vow seems to offer an eventual escape from that tension: "...until we are parted by death."

But who knows about the death part?

How about divorce? Seemed a remote issue, about other couples, until I got divorced. Sometimes people getting married for a second time ask me, "How can you make that vow twice in the same lifetime?"

Good question. I've experienced that discomfort. The formal, legal marriage may end, but some piece of it never totally ends. It's indelible, beyond conscious control; can't be severed. Something beyond our willful decision-making had a hand in creating it. Uncomfortable for me to consider—despite being wonderfully married again, this time for more than 40 years—that something in me recognized that indelible connection when I married the first time. I guess I was not ready to do the work it required. And grateful I could end the marriage, if not the piece of me that remains connected.

After I explained all that to a couple getting remarried, the woman smiled indulgently. "Well, maybe that's true for some," she said, "but Frank and I were married barely a year, parted amicably, and have no lingering connections."

"Well then," I said, "you won't mind my inviting Frank for our next session so you and he can be sure to have finished all the issues between you."

"Bull shit!" she interjected. "You have no right . . ."

"Yes, bull shit," I admitted. "I just wanted us all to acknowledge the piece of a relationship that will always own us."

I think she forgave me, reluctantly.

I'd like to think I'm getting closer to forgiving myself for having left my first marriage with precious little examining of what of it is permanently embedded in me. And I am grateful to have grown enough to be able to own the rich and poor, better and worse, in a wonderful 40-year, and counting, marriage.

That's my understanding of sacrament: something that owns a piece of us. Rich, complex, largely beneath our conscious. It can be comforting. And discomforting. Nonnegotiable.

So many mysteries lay claim to us. We're only vaguely aware of most of them. They remain mysteries until they unexpectedly, almost always uninvited, find a way to show themselves.

Might I have chosen priesthood, hoping to have an inside track to these mysteries? In fact, the mysteries have only deepened over the years since I set out on that path. Surely one function of religion is to make us come to terms with the reality of how much of life is beyond our control or understanding. Is it an essential piece of what's required to become comfortable in our own skin?

I fantasize that when people see me coming, they say to themselves, "Just a simple 'Good Morning.' Don't mention dying, or I'll be here all afternoon."

Am I really that weird? Yeah, probably.

Prayer?

Maybe prayer is what we do when our usual ways of coping can't contain emotion, fear, doubts that are too powerful for us to manage.

Dan Rather asked Mother Teresa what she said when she prayed.

"I listen."

"And what does God say?"

"Oh, God listens too."

My younger sister, Perry, a multi-year cancer survivor, has taught me a lot about carrying mortality lightly while living fully. As counselor and hospital chaplain, she has been a big help to people wrestling with terminal illness.

On my 78th birthday, the age at which my father and older sister each died, Perry said, "Your job is to have another birthday."

Four years later, and counting. Being born is the most surprising and fascinating thing that happens to us, until we die.

Death as Ecstasy

I imagine that dying may be ecstasy, once the ego's terror of losing control loosens its grip.

Probably the closest we come to dying until we expel that last breath is during sex. Orgasm. For that ecstatic moment we lose our boundaries, give ourselves to the other, in a rare sense of being one with everything. It's fleeting, elusive. And for most of us one of life's most memorable moments.

The Spanish call orgasm, *La Muerte Pequeña*, The Little Death—our lifelong struggle between control and letting go, resolved in a moment's unscheduled ecstasy.

Here I am, wrestling this enigma into the surprise old age is turning out to be.

Death-fascination may be a particularly natural focus for a priest who is helping usher so many into eternity. Do stockbrokers wonder a lot about death while building portfolios for the future? Maybe only undertakers spend as much time with it.

When I met my new doctor a few years ago he asked, "So what can I do for you?"

"If it goes the way I hope," I answered, "all you'll ever have to do for me is pronounce me dead."

He smiled. "A minimalist, huh?"

Within the limits of his Hippocratic Oath, he has honored that. And he surely knows I sounded braver than I am, and that I reserve the right to be terrified.

Who knows whether I'm whistling past the graveyard or have actually gained at least tentative confidence from years of tending people's deaths?

Our conscious/unconscious has been compared to an iceberg, 90% below the surface, 10% above.

Weird, all the things we catch ourselves doing, thinking, unaware they had been lurking in us, like, when I wiggle my nose to work my glasses back up when they slide down. It's a trick I learned as a very little boy. I was born with a lazy eye. Though surgery eventually corrected it, I wore glasses from 18 months until late adolescence. Had each eye patched before corrective surgery. When I concentrate, I squint, despite having pretty good eyesight for my age. These things slip into our habits and we are mostly unaware of them.

How has early compromised sight—glasses, eyes patched—affected what I see when I look out at the world?

Lacey would tell you I don't see clutter. Especially my own. Or color subtleties. Design. Her acute, finely-honed, interior-designer sense influences how the world looks to her. Living with her has sharpened my picture of the world. But how much do I continue to filter the world through what my eight-year-old eyes saw?

We say that, as children, our feelings and emotions are less measured, more immediately available. Sadness, excitement, fear, and confusion, are emotions we learn to keep under wraps as grownups. Presumably it is on behalf of living as orderly, unchaotic a day as we can. That can leave us out of touch with an emotive dimension that is as essential a piece of us as those for which the world gives us a bigger payoff.

In old age, those filters seem to become more porous. For good and for ill. Spontaneous crying, fits of rage, owning up to confusion and weakness, rise more quickly to the surface. No wonder old age can seem like a second childhood—and make us anxious since we're so powerfully conditioned to keep all that quiet.

As I age, new demands ascend the hierarchy of concerns: learning to sleep again, move my bowels, tame my once ambitious hunger for success, approval. Eventually our bodies' demands outsmart our learned motivations.

A Bit of Wishful Thinking

Conrad, a close friend, while dying of metastatic melanoma, showed me that dying can be holy and fulfilling. His body was gradually shutting down and he used the remaining time to say goodbye and thank people he loved.

Not many years ago, he was my mentor in bike riding and many other things. He was a much more experienced, stronger rider than I am. He'd call midday to set up a ride and I'd try to weasel out of it because I didn't think I could keep up with him. He refused to let me off the hook and I was always grateful because I would discover I was stronger than I ever thought I'd be.

He faced dying with steadfast serenity. I wonder if I will be able to follow him in that. He reassured me in the same way he did while we were riding.

Even so, I continue to wonder, worry, fear. My smart body carries on breathing without my conscious assistance. Precious commodity, breath, with a best-buy date. I'm a lazy meditator, easily distracted. Still learning the healing power of measured breathing. After all these years of sporadic meditating, I keep on keeping on.

Conrad persists; stays with me on far more than just every bike ride. But I know it's a bit of wishful thinking, projection, and just plain denial, to expect anyone to go gently.

Conrad refused a hospital bed because he wanted to die in his own bed—his wife was lying next to him, along with his favorite cat. His final couple of days were tough. As much as it's possible to know, he seemed free of pain and wasn't afraid.

I recently read a book, *How To Change Your Mind* by Michael Pollan, a brave adventurer who experimented with psychedelic therapy. He lost himself in those out-of-body moments, experienced his own non-being. He found it terrifying—and exhilarating (maybe like orgasm?). Terrifying, because it was a palpable taste of dying, not being. Exhilarating, because he found the experience totally trustworthy. At least for that moment he lost his fear of death. It no longer mattered whether there was something or nothing.

Do I dare believe that's what it will be like to give away that final exhale? No need to struggle for another inhale?

Do you?

For better or for worse, terrifying or wonderful, that exhale will accomplish the letting go we talk so much about. My body overruling my mind. My fear. Even shutting down my body's autonomic nervous system, tasked with keeping me alive. What will that be like?

Ecstasy?

As I look back, my life's direction looks more like a course sailed by a drunk than a point-to-point course.

I've learned to be a little more generous with myself, more willing to forgive my missteps. That ability to forgive ourselves, embrace what is, what has been, let go of regret, becomes a measure of how much we can let ourselves find pleasure in getting old.

It comes and goes.

Who Gets to Decide?

Grownup responsibility can be unnerving. Sometimes life asks us to surrender to demands we couldn't have imagined.

In my first post, I became friends with the Assistant DA in Summit County, Ohio. Stephan was smart, funny, brave, fierce. Spending time with him was a big high for me.

One day I found him sitting on his living room floor surrounded by open books.

Shakespeare's complete works, Thesaurus, Bible.

"What's up, Stephan?" I asked.

"I'm putting together the punishment phase of the trial we're finishing. Asking for the death penalty."

Something about the calm, dispassionate manner of this caring, sensitive man constructing an argument for killing someone, unsettled me.

"I read about that in the paper, Stephan. I thought your boss was trying that case."

"He doesn't believe in the death penalty, so when we get to this phase he has me do it."

"You *do* believe in the death penalty?"

"I'm the assistant DA. The law provides for the death penalty in a murder-one verdict. I've told my boss he should resign if he doesn't want to do this."

"Man, that's hard-ass, Stephan. I know you as compassionate. Must take its toll."

"It's my job. Every job requires hard things."

That was nearly 60 years ago. I admired Stephan. We marched together for civil rights, fair housing, anti-Vietnam War.

The thought of willing someone, whatever we may think of what they have done, to die, intentionally, legally, stirs deep dread in me.

A rabbi once told me he didn't understand the Christian notion of God's unconditional forgiveness. "We believe forgiveness requires setting right the wrong. Since we can't restore life, taking a life can't be forgiven. At least by us."

I never asked Stephan if he felt he was responsible for the man's death, or if he was able to consider it simply doing his duty.

Did he imagine he was helping complete God's work, resetting the moral compass? A life for a life? The ancient code Christians claim Jesus has made mute. What's it like to stand in for God in such a weighty matter?

What did it cost Stephan to ask the jury to vote for the death penalty? What did it cost members of the jury?

We give this awesome authority to some people. Not being one of them, I don't think I can know what it's like to be put in that position.

Whose Meaning?

Is it because I try to portray what the unknowable God is up to, that I straddle that line between what's mine to decide, and what lies beyond me? How to pry open that gate between conscious and unconscious beneath? No owner's manual. Who do I think I am? We're the meaning makers. Working it out as we go along. Always reaching for what, like Tantalus' reach for water and fruit, seems always just beyond our grasp.

Sometimes after reading "Zone Note," the short email pieces I send most Tuesdays, someone texts: "You lost me. What's it supposed to mean?"

"Supposed to mean? It's not supposed to mean anything except how it grabs you." I respond. "*You* tell *me* what it means. I'm hoping to point to a piece of the mystery I'm trying to unravel. Hoping you'll help with something you see that I haven't."

Life's mysteries deepen as it nears its completion. The stakes become less theoretical. More elusive, maybe less urgent? Love to think so.

With thoughts urgent or elusive, we are all circling the ancient enigma: God.

Every discipline has its peculiarities. Surgeons are fascinated by what's covered by skin. Computer programmers by whatever algorithms are. Theologians by what our minds, even at their most agile, find beyond reach of our powers.

The Vocation of Weird

Though we like to be considered rational, we're a weird, archaic guild.

John Coburn, dean of my seminary, later my bishop, talked about many clergy who express frustration because no one treats us like "normal" people.

"Normal?" John laughed. "We spend years deciphering documents from centuries ago, that the rest of the world has long forgotten. Dress in archaic costume, kneel in obedience to undemocratic authority. Sing when prose fails us. (Augustine: "Who sings, prays twice.") Stand in a pulpit, high above people, sponsoring unseen, ineffable realms as if we have privileged access to them. Like meaning, suffering, dying. Preside at ceremony that conjures a martyr who died and is in some way yet alive. Whose death and new life somehow contain the means to the life we long for.

That amorphous "Somehow," is the fuel that runs the engine we're supposed to keep well-tuned.

"And then complain that we aren't treated like normal people?"

Normal turns out to be what I imagine you must be, and I'm not.

If Not Normal, What?

This fiction/cross-millennium memoir, travels the rutted road of revelation.

Revelation—reveal. The most revealing moments I experience in exchanges with people are when they tell me a story about something that has great meaning to them. A story revealing the source of their passion, their power.

That's the kindness you're paying me: sitting still long enough for me tell you my stories.

The Bible, Hebrew, Greek, human stories are all packed with meaning: the Gilgamesh flood story; Moses on the mountain. Human stories offering glimpses of life, saturated with the ineffable: Buddha under the Bodhi tree, George Washington on the Delaware, Abraham Lincoln at Gettysburg, 9/11, Dr. King, portraying his dream before hundreds of thousands of eager seekers. Covid 19. Barack Obama's health care. Donald Trump and the January 6, 2021, attack on the Capital. Putin invading Ukraine.

Stories become legend. Their power becomes greater as we become animated in the telling. It's our story, conceived in mystery, sometimes leaching into the conscious tier, worth exploring. Its significance extending beyond the details.

Having exhausted every conscious, rational idea or image I can conceive, trying to explain to myself what we're doing here, I sometimes turn to singing. Psalms. Hymns. Elvis. Leonard Cohen. I read poetry to myself, aloud, listening for a voice that's borrowing mine that may lead to dimensions beyond what my rational mind can construct.

Then there's the elusive meditating. Sitting through ego-mind's relentless detours. Occasionally sensing your body signaling something powerful and unnameable.

Daydreaming, whistling. Humming. Things we do without being aware, that can sometimes elude ego's determination to keep us in its bondage.

Every tradition has forms intended to wean us from thinking we're meant to be in charge. We encounter them from earliest days. Fairy tales, legends, myths. Songs. If you're steeped in Christian worship, maybe it's a phrase like:

Praise God from whom all blessings flow . . .

If Jewish, maybe:

How is this night different from other nights?

It conjures a host of feelings. Its cadence becomes embedded in consciousness.

Can an ancient formula gain traction in people not steeped in the tradition it comes from?

That question haunts me. Surely parochial boundaries don't have to preclude our finding common ground in searching for meaning. Can the hymns, Bible stories, ceremonies, so familiar to me, make sense, matter, even if you weren't raised with them?

God, or whatever name you give to what matters most, what is ineffable, indescribable, is what I've spent most of my life trying to point to, find words to describe.

Is it a preacher's fantasy to think I might channel a voice that can maybe use mine? My voice, my energy, my imagination, being used to help you hear that small voice within your own voice.

Yes, trying to remain alert to that voice, even though we must never forget it can serve up wishful, self-serving bullshit. But keeping silent seems like admitting defeat. Thinking that the rational voice that speaks to us in our own idiom is all we can know, leaves us emotionally and spiritually impoverished.

So let's speak, you and I, with as much confidence as we can muster.

Jesus, Gandhi, Martin Luther King, Jr., Buddha, went out on that fragile, bending limb, betting the ranch on the integrity of the quest, defying just about everything human culture seems intent on instilling in us: fear, suspicion, and doubt that puts us on guard against each other. Against our eyes being opened to what we are conditioned to not see.

Most of us aren't instinctively brave in standing against what everything in our culture—in collusion with ego—says isn't real. I'm mostly not so brave. But I'm hungry for that elusive dimension, and at 82, I don't have a lot of time to rebuild my courage.

Jesus, Gandhi, MLK, faced the consequences of being faithful to a vision that challenges assumptions, prejudices.

Every one of them, assassinated.

I wonder if, by the time you read this, Volodymyr Zelenskyy will still be alive? The sheer force of his imagination, refusal to accept what the world said was certain immediate defeat, has added another chapter to human certainty being overturned by the seemingly impossible. His standing firm against heartless violence, knowing the odds against him, has made further inroads into what we all believed we knew about what would happen.

Most of us aren't faced with anything that scary, until we are. Letting our hidden places see light, leading from our vulnerable, undefended selves is its own form of dying. Dying to dreams of presenting an impressive, invulnerable self.

My vocation, the human vocation, is learning to trust, to lower our defenses against mystery. Some invoke the holy name, some not.

Jacob wrestles all night with an angel (Genesis 32), as we do on those long sleepless nights. In the morning, exhausted, he begs the angel to let him go. Before leaving, the angel touches Jacob on his inner thigh (scrotum?), his regenerative place, dislocating his hip, leaving him marked, permanently wounded. Bearing a new identity, Israel, which means, "I wrestled with God and lived." But not without a wound.

No matter what we "believe," we wrestle with God, with what to do with knowing we belong to something bigger than our ego awareness. Knowing we're always in over our depth, leaves us with a wound to our ego, our dream of autonomy. As it did Jacob. A seeming imperfection, a reminder we're incomplete, unfinished until something beyond us completes us.

It's as if I wake mornings having heard that voice: *I know you're tired, discouraged, but I'm not done with you yet.*

Venturing. Learning to see beyond the boundaries I erect, seeking safety.

Embracing imperfection, my need for you. All my life I've wrestled with wanting to hide that part of me that feels so vulnerable.

That weakness, my Achilles Heel, is the portal through which my best self can emerge. Not the in-charge man, but the indigent one: needy, unexpectedly resourceful.

It is a work in progress: assembling, reassembling.

We're here for a glorious magical season that finds its completion in surrendering dreams of personal perfection.

On my best days I embrace my imperfection.

Maybe there's a way to have more best days.

Bumpy road crowded with obstacles, most of our own making.

A road laced with wonder.

This morning, a bird outside my window was loudly singing the most gorgeous tune. Where did she learn that tune? Can my heart drop its skepticism so that song might give me a taste of that bird's rapture? What does that bird know that elicits from her that transporting song every daybreak?

I have occasionally experienced the liberating discovery of sensing in everyone, everything I meet, an invitation. An invitation to connect with that elusive reality I'm so eager for. The sense that I'm more like an atom in a molecule than the whole molecule.

It's about discovering and nurturing connections. Everything connected to everything. Everyone to everyone.

A Zen Story

A man walking along the swollen Ganges sees an old monk, precariously perched on a tree limb, hanging over the rushing current. As he watches, the monk reaches out to a scorpion about to be swept off a rock.

He watches as the monk reached once, twice, three times, each time the scorpion swings up its tail and stings him. The man's face is grotesquely swollen from the stings.

"You! Stupid old man!" he shouts at the monk. "Don't you know that scorpion will sting you every time you reach for it?"

The monk turns and considers the man.

"Because it is in the scorpion's nature to sting, must I surrender my nature to save?"

Our true nature?

Comforting, discomforting, never totally free of anxiety, the choice keeps offering itself. Our bodies, consciousness, ego unaware, are in fact tuned to it. It's like breathing oxygen.

Perverse, that I have the capacity—even, it seems, the inclination—to choose against my best design.

Do dogs, otters, have ego? Do they ever choose against their own best interest?

We may not—likely won't—recognize when we choose for God, embrace the Buddha, transcend ego, make room for more spacious reality. We're mercifully unaware of the countless complex transactions our bodies are continually negotiating to help us do just that.

Whether we sign up for it or not, our bodies will one day outsmart our ego to take us on an exhilarating ride.

Hang on.

Shaping Starts Early: Manly Domination

I was eight. My father, a salesman, going on a trip of several days, knelt in front of me, putting us at equal eye level.

"I'll be gone a few days. You'll be the man of the house." I nodded solemnly. Flattered? Certainly perplexed. What about my mother, older sister? Pretty savvy younger sister, too. Age, gender, as yet unexamined gauges of hierarchy, authority.

Domination. Birthright. Well-born, White, male, has always felt like a heavy weight. Coming to recognize the legitimate authority of the seemingly least among us has been a lifelong spiritual discipline.

Racism

Again, eight years old. My father overheard me respond to Gertrude, our Black maid, whom I cherished as warm, nurturing, mother figure:

"Yes, M'am."

Later, Dad took me aside. Gently explained, "Son, you don't call a colored woman, 'M'am'. It's not polite. Embarrasses her."

He also explained that our revered family doctor said the reason Black boxers usually defeated White boxers on the Friday night fights on TV, was because Negroes have thicker skulls. Presumably, smaller brain cavities.

Racism, national plague. So much for nurturing connections. Another manifestation of our species' self-sabotage.

My father, family standard bearer, set the bar for me, the only son. Patriarchy. Racism.

What I didn't discover until grown, was how deep my roots go into the antebellum south.

I'd heard my father talk, a little, about his father's family in Sewanee, Tennessee. Seems his grandfather, an emigree from England, who failed trying to farm in Iowa, traveled to Sewanee where, immediately following the Civil War he had a hand in founding the University of the South.

My cousin Jo Colmore, who raises Salers cattle in Rising Fawn, Georgia, just over the mountain from Sewanee, emailed me that it's unthinkable that a Colmore would never have visited Sewanee.

Lacey agreed to go with me on that surreal pilgrimage.

The University was like a Colmore haunted house. The Chancellor even showed us the christening gowns that had belonged to my great aunts, two maiden ladies remembered by graduates from the 1940s and 50s as housemothers in fraternities.

It was unsettling to wonder how much of the genteel—and not so genteel—south may yet inhabit my bones. Not that my upper-middle-class upbringing in the north wasn't infused with the racism that's part of every White American.

It sometimes feels that bar might yet crush me. Not until long grown did I grasp the extent of the weight of racism and chauvinism in me. Burdens I was trained to carry as if they were marks of my superiority. I don't think I ever experienced them as the privilege they're often portrayed as being for White, middle-class men. They became liabilities I tried to excise. More conditioning that divided me from people whose life experience was different. A piece of the cultural system that encouraged me to assume authority over people, precluding the possibility of intimacy I have longed for, what I suspect we all long for. To dare to love each other, which requires us to let our soft underbelly be exposed. To dare to have connections.

Early Mentor

Our parish rector, Henry Rightor, a stylish, folksy, charismatic preacher from Helena, Arkansas (and, I've long wondered, my mother's lover?), spent a portion of his charisma trying—cautiously, futilely—to wean his parishioners, fellow southerners, from embedded racism.

Like Gertrude, he was extravagantly compassionate, egalitarian when measured against other males in authority I knew.

Birdie, my beagle, followed me across the road and was crushed to death by a car. Gertrude came running, pulled me off the bloodied corpse, carried me inside, went back, scraped Birdie off the road. Called Mr. Rightor.

"You got to come, right *now!*"

He spent the afternoon with Gertrude and me. I asked him if Birdie would go to heaven.

"Do you love Birdie?"

"Yes, a lot," I whimpered.

"Your love for Birdie and Birdie's for you, means you'll always be together, even after you both die. Nothing can kill the love that joins you together."

That story is lodged in a place in me that endures. The stuff from which vocations are formed.

Secret Liberals

My father was a business man: Republican. My mother, quietly in cahoots with Mr. Rightor, who was, by White, middle-class, southern measure at the time, a liberal Democrat.

Nineteen-fifty-two: Eisenhower, running for president, came to Charlotte. Did a telethon.

My mother and Mr. Rightor put me up to calling in. An 11-year-old voice might get a response? The question they gave me: *Why have you not repudiated Senator McCarthy?*

Did I know Senator McCarthy had bullied and lied himself into a position of abusive power from which he wreaked havoc? Years later a friend told me his Jewish, Communist, talented, screen-writer father, was blacklisted by Hollywood. The violence Senator McCarthy's demagoguery made on his family drove him out of Hollywood. A prefiguring of 21st century American politics.

I sensed it was a daring question Mom and Mr. Rightor put me up to in the hierarchical, 1952 south. I think I was excited that we were in effect challenging a national bully.

I was fascinated, puzzled, by Mr. Rightor's unconventional job; persona, vestments, sacraments, humor, pushing cautiously against the prevailing culture. He took my child-grief seriously, much the way I have come to think about Jesus' compassion. He considered my passive mother at least as important as my aggressive, over-achieving father. As I look back, I think it began there. My vocation. Life choice.

It came as a surprise years later, when I found those early-life experiences drawing me toward ordination.

Despite powerful conditioning about who counts— White, assertive male—I sensed it was a bad fit for me. Maybe I knew, early on, I would never be assertive, confident enough, to pull it off.

But before I could hope to break free, I had to acknowledge the strong hold that conditioning had on me.

Curious, sorting through early moments, coming across memories that seemed insignificant at the time that may have shaped life choices.

Non-Vocation

First day in seventh-grade shop. Mr. Leith gave us each a simple task: something to assemble, get a sense of our ability using our hands.

When he came to me, looked at whatever I had tried to do, he said, "Colmore, you're going to be shop foreman."

"What's the foreman do?" I asked.

"Pretty much nothing. You'll oversee others' work."

I understood I'd best not try to shape my life around mostly absent manual skills.

Probably like most preachers, I've always loved words. And abstractions.

My mother, Mr. Rightor, Bill Schenck—so many people who influenced me—loved words.

Choosing wasn't simple. A lot of energy went into trying to compensate for skills I lacked, and feared were required to be considered an accomplished man.

Only now, years later, do I see more clearly choices I tried to make, deferring to my conditioning, denying my heart. Subverting what I unknowingly longed for.

Those memories can be painful.

Lacking Courage

1967: LOOKING FOR A HOUSE
IN WASHINGTON, D.C.

After being shown several we liked but couldn't afford, the realtor took us to a new area. She showed us a lovely house in a very nice neighborhood. Price tag significantly lower than others we'd seen.

As we drove away, I expressed excitement about the house. She said, "There's one thing I have to explain. You would be the first White people to live here since the neighborhood went Black many years ago."

It was clearly an upper-middle-class neighborhood, ordinarily beyond our financial reach.

We talked about it at some length. Decided we weren't quite ready to make such a radical choice, be a minority.

Now, more than fifty-years later, I regret not having understood I was being given a chance to put my money where my mouth was. A chance to live with people different from me. Grow. All these years later

Only now, years later, do I see more clearly choices I tried to make, deferring to my conditioning, denying my heart. Subverting what I unknowingly longed for.

Those memories can be painful.

Graddy's Cross

My maternal grandfather was Dean of the Episcopal Cathedral of Havana before being named Bishop of Puerto Rico. I saw him only a handful of times before he died, when I was ten. I have a foggy memory of him. His legacy among his children, my father and his sisters and brothers, gave him oversize weight in family lore.

I'll always wonder how much that lore seeped into my bones. Maybe I understood that when I told my father I was going to seminary, whatever his disappointment about my not seeking a more lucrative, competitive, commercial role, would yield to his admiration for, maybe even be slightly intimidated by, my following his revered father's life choice.

Shortly after I was ordained a priest, my Aunt Sarah sent me her father's pectoral cross, the symbol of his office as bishop. Uncertain whether it was appropriate for a mere priest to wear a bishop's cross, it lay in a drawer for many years until a colleague assured me it wasn't presumptuous.

It felt powerful to hang it around my neck when I led worship. Maybe a bow to my conditioning to climb the hierarchy?

A decade or so after I retired, the recently retired Presiding Bishop of the United States, Katharine Jefferts-Schori—first female primate, another challenge to historical male hierarchy—was Interim Bishop of San Diego. When she visited St. James, my former parish, I asked her if she knew Griselda Delgado del Carpio, the newly elected Bishop of Cuba.

It was only in the late 20th century that ordination was opened to women in the Anglican/Episcopal Church. That the highest position in the American church should be a woman, and even more so in a traditionally male-dominated culture like Cuba, was initially mind boggling. The wheels of change normally grind slowly in the church, but the pace at which women have made their way into every level is astonishing.

I am finding it thrilling.

Bishop Katharine did know Bishop Griselda (wonderful that women bishops welcome their title being followed by their given name, rather than by their father's or spouse's family name). She spoke warmly of her, hoped Bishop Griselda might make it to the next meeting of the American House of Bishops.

"If I give you my grandfather's pectoral cross," I asked Bishop Katharine, "do you think you could give it to Bishop Griselda? Explain my grandfather was once Dean of her cathedral before becoming Bishop of Puerto Rico."

Two months later Bishop Katharine sent me a photo of Bishop Griselda proudly holding my grandfather's pectoral cross.

In some mysterious way that confirmed another layer of my vocation. Though I was retired, it lent me a small place in affirming women in a role men had exclusively occupied. Collegiality trumping hierarchy, another echo of the life Jesus' urges us to embrace. Another chipping away at the structures that have kept us from the intimacy we hunger for.

My grandfather's pectoral cross, hanging from Griselda's neck, makes my heart sing a tune I hadn't heard.

My sense of Bishop Katharine, and even the remote connection with Bishop Griselda, was about more than the justice of it. The experience of sitting with Katharine at lunch was of a different order from times I've spent with male bishops. It set me wondering.

I experienced a rich time with a generous-spirited friend. Not someone who outranked me in the hierarchy (thought without question she did outrank me). Hard to pinpoint precisely what fed that sense. But fifty years of life in ecclesiastical hierarchy made me feel the difference unmistakably.

All these years later, out of the loop almost as long as I was in it, moments like that continue to reshape my understanding of the vocation that still has a hold on me.

Nana and Cuba

Curious, that Sylvia Angel de Murias, my maternal grandmother, was from Cuba. So far as I know, Nana and Graddy, maternal grandmother and fraternal grandfather, both of whom spent a significant piece of their lives in the Caribbean, never met until their children married.

Nana died when I was 5. She too held legendary status in my mother's family. After she married Albert Vander Veer—my mother's father, from a Dutch/ Albany family—she lived out her days in New York City. But it seems life on the upper-east-side of Manhattan didn't erode her Latin love of poking fun at the stiff culture she married into. Her puncturing of proper façade kept Papa off balance and delighted my mother.

She and my father loved speaking Spanish to each other because Nana spoke proper Castilian Spanish, while Dad spoke the colloquial tongue of Puerto Rico.

The irony of my legacy came full circle when we spent summers at Papa Vander Veer's summer house on

Fire Island. Our cook, Felicia, was Puerto Rican. Dad would leave the dinner table, slip away from the many cocktail parties, and sit at the kitchen table speaking the kind of Spanish he grew up speaking.

Visiting us in La Jolla, he sought out Mexicans, ubiquitous in southern California, to speak Spanish with.

One of his first visits, he stopped to speak with a man doing work in a well-groomed garden. When he rejoined us he said, "How nice to find people who speak proper Spanish."

In 2011, Lacey and I went to Cuba. The decaying remnants of once beautiful, rich, Havana weren't merely of interest because of Nana's family—sugar cane and tobacco plantation owners—were among the very rich, Spanish colonialists.

In addition to visiting my ancestors' elaborate gravesite in Colon cemetery, we visited a museum that collected artifacts from before Castro's revolution.

"Look at that!" Lacey said, as we passed a case of dining-room china from colonial days. We recognized Nana's family china, identical to a set shelved in our old farmhouse in Vermont.

Maybe the many cultures that inhabit my blood explain why I'll never have a strong sense of belonging to some parochial group. The tribe I belong to is the human tribe. Or, in the days when we liked to brag about immigrants from all over making the United States, were we more united? How sad this extraordinary mixture is now being portrayed as threat.

Sophomore Spirituality
Unlikely Beginning

Freshman year in college, a friend, drunk, had a telephone fight with his girlfriend, threw the phone through his dorm room window, came looking for me. Why me? We weren't particularly close friends. From my high-rise room, I heard him calling me.

I went down. We walked the cold, rainy streets of West Philadelphia mostly in silence. We came to a church with a red door (Episcopal churches in Philadelphia had red doors), went in, and sat on a long bench. I pulled out a prayer book (also red), and I must have read aloud, though I don't remember what. Stumbled our way through the Lord's Prayer.

Years later when my seminary in Cambridge absorbed the Philadelphia Divinity School, I realized we had been in the seminary chapel. Sometimes it seems I was being summoned by a vocation I had yet to identify.

After a half-hour or so, he seemed sober, said he'd be all right. We walked back to the dorms, went to our separate rooms. (His must have been cold with the broken window).

The next morning, as I left my room for an 8 A.M. Spanish class, he was in the hall, waiting.

"I don't know what last night was about," he said, "but I'd just as soon you didn't tell anyone. I mean to forget it ever happened."

I promised not to tell, but I've never forgotten about it.

It was an adolescent moment, hardly a conversion that wouldn't pass muster with Jonathan Edwards. Was there some lasting significance to his having sought me out? I thought so. Still do.

Feeling set aside for a purpose—in this case, compassionate attention—is tricky. It's also what we mean by vocation: "A strong feeling of suitability for a particular career or occupation." (Oxford Dictionary.)

Vocation can feel noble. Though because of it's obvious appeal to ego's self-importance, it can be mixed with ignobility.

Childhood in the segregated south has left me with the uncomfortable reality of the legacy of racism that infects our nation, and I have to confess, endures in my darker angel. I will go to my grave seeing dark skin a marker in ways white skin doesn't. Once it signaled to me a person, likely less sophisticated, if not less intelligent. Like many White liberals in the years since the Civil Rights Revolution, I can still find myself overcompensating, being more solicitous than I might with a White person under similar circumstance.

Racism isn't the only prejudice once, not even recognized as prejudice, with a claim on me.

And, Yes, Anti-Semitism

LEGACY AND HIERARCHY

Dinner with my cousin Julie at a restaurant on East End Avenue, NYC, May, 1965. Julie was an editor at Viking Press: beautiful, sophisticated, fun. She tried to teach me how to navigate the big city, but it never took. I am intimidated by the city to this day.

Julie was dating a man she told me she loved. I listened to her describe a caring, gentle man with whom she shared a love of books, art, food. She said he'd asked her to marry him. But she wasn't sure.

"Why not?" I wondered.

"He's Jewish."

"So?"

"Blayney, do you know how many Jewish members the Bedford Golf & Tennis Club has?"

"How many?"

"None."

"But, Julie, you live in the City, not Bedford."

"Mum and Dad live in Bedford. I've never taken him to their house."

"Come on, Julie, this is the 20th century."

Julie smiled indulgently.

"OK," she said, "if you're so liberated, how about we each take off our Colmore signet rings, and throw them into the East River. Renounce our heritage."

"Don't be ridiculous, Julie, you can marry him without throwing your ring in the river."

She took hers off, put it on the table between us.

"You throw yours in and I'll throw mine."

I didn't. Neither did Julie. She never married him. Nor anyone. She died young, of a stroke. I still miss her. She tested my resolve for justice, and found it wanting.

I still have that ring, wear it for dress-up.

No doubt I know many more Jews now than I did then. The club I belong to in La Jolla has its share. Largely Jews well integrated into WASP culture.

My inclinations toward old prejudice persists, stubbornly.

More than 40 years, husband of a strong, fiercely independent woman, with accomplished daughters and a step-daughter, gender parity has become for me as much survival strategy as conviction. Not to mention fending off the sense of being among the elite, responsible for all manner of things. My saner self recognizes how ridiculous that is.

Infected by male hierarchy, racism, anti-Semitism, classism, plagues I've learned to curb, but never totally leach from my psyche.

Sophomore year, fraternity member, fraternity rushing. Long debates about who fits. One person most of us thought a perfect fit. But one member had concerns about his "pedigree."

"I think his grandfather may have been Jewish." Lots of furrowed brows. One person, from the same town as the potential member, volunteered to do some sleuthing.

"Really?" I asked. "We all agree he'd make a good member, but we might turn him down because he has a Jewish grandfather?" It was the first time I had spoken during the evening. I was among the newest, youngest members. Surprised to have dared voice an opinion.

"Don't be so naïve," I was told, "it's not just about him. It's about opening the fraternity to a whole new group who would never fit."

My courage faltered. I shut up. After a sleepless night, I decided to take my absence from the fraternity. Had I been braver, I might have stuck around and tried to help change things. Others must have, because I have learned they now welcome, not only Jews, but women. Unthinkable then.

When someone asks when I decided to become a priest, that rainy, cold night in West Philadelphia, 60 years ago springs to mind. Along with the antisemitism in that fraternity-rush meeting. And Gertrude and Mr. Rightor devoting an afternoon to my trauma over Birdie's death. And maybe the thrill of being a part of puncturing Senator McCarthy's pompous prejudice.

It wouldn't require a skilled therapist to read into my vocation a longing to count, to matter. And to set right the wrongs I learned as a child. Easy to become cynical, but what are our lives made of except these stories? And how they weighted the choices we made.

Having listened to countless stories from people troubled by whether their lives have made any difference, I have reassured them that my life choices, understood in retrospect, have come from small, often ignoble moments that awakened my hunger for compassion. And to make connections I would once have eschewed.

How to Satisfy
the Hierarchy

The irony is that in order to gain credentials for being "licensed" to take a leadership role in following the radically egalitarian Jesus, I had to satisfy the constraints of the Episcopal hierarchy.

Canonical examiners are guardians of our post-enlightenment, priestly guild against excessive eccentricity, straying too far from consensus orthodoxy. Or that's how I perceived the questions they asked about what motivated me to seek ordination. Following intuition, trusting emotion, can be disruptive to organized religion. Or organized anything. I told the examiners about how reading Teilhard de Chardin, Nikos Kazantzakis, showed me new dimensions of reality. I guess that satisfied my examiners even if it didn't send electricity through my bones like that day in Charlotte, or that night freshman year.

Maybe it's a false dichotomy, intellect versus intuition. Like distinctions we make between body and mind.

Linear, rational intellect can make us suspicious of unsettling passion even though they both inhabit a single being. I wonder if our radar can be recalibrated, granting equal authority to passion and reason?

Writing in year 81, I see things take new shape. Zinnia, our Norfolk terrier, just turned 8. The night before her birthday, I dreamed we were scattering her ashes in the stone wall in Vermont where 10 years ago we scattered her predecessor, Cosmos', ashes. I woke with a deep sense of loss. My attachment to these dogs has become more intense as I've grown older. Akin perhaps to a growing affection for infants (*enfant*—Middle English—not speaking). No longer distractions from weightier matters, but bearers of a less guarded love that I might once have dismissed as sentimental. If our species is to enjoy an extended tenure, we might rediscover our place alongside, rather than above, our fellow species. I love considering it's not we who have domesticated dogs, but dogs who have domesticated us.

It's said that when cats and dogs realized that overbearing, humans seemed determined to become the planet's dominant species they held a powwow to consider the best strategy for coping.

The dogs said since it seemed inevitable the smartest choice would be to adapt, go along, let humans believe they were in charge. It also meant dogs could mostly rest, rarely have to hunt for food, and be comfortably housed. Yes, it required toadying up to them, which, while sometimes humiliating, seemed better than constant conflict.

"Fuck that!" the cats said, "We refuse to pretend to be domesticated just to satisfy their insatiable appetite for power. We remain feral, and they'll just have to deal with that."

And so it has been.

Our children think it's funny that in our old age, we have the most high-maintenance terrier of the four I have known. Maybe because she demands so much of my energy, refuses to give in to my efforts to calm her, I think I'm even more attached to her than those who have gone before.

Might she live five more years? Outlive me?

Our children, seeing my raw grief when one of our animal's dies, wondered if I had lost my grip. It might have shaken their view of my being the in-control adult. I hope that has proved helpful in their giving expression to their own grief.

The kind of grief I had witnessed among Black Africans, rarely among Middle-class American Episcopalians, can claim a piece of me that I usually have kept at arm's length. After all, I was the priest, the shaman, who exuded calm reassurance.

Our terriers love us the way we wish we could love each other, not seeming to notice all the things about me that make me unlovable. Why wouldn't they also reach a place of grief deep in us?

Recent Land Dwellers

As I've aged, my love of swimming, especially ocean swimming, has grown from simple recreation to a sense of being embraced by our ancient Mother. Whether primordial or womb memory, or both, something about salt water—so close to human blood plasma, and less burdened by gravity—reinforces a sense in me that may be vestigial.

That sense is stamped in a place that can be hard to access.

It may be that those without agency in the competition for power—infants, aging people, mentally ill, deep introverts, people on the spectrum—wake the counter-cultural conviction that power that endures, and resides not in achievement, but simply in existence, can make simply being here seem a gift. Imagine if we could recapture the surprise it must have been to emerge from our mother's warm, dark belly, having to breathe, adjust to light, gravity. Or becoming aware of the odds—against reality of there being something here where for billions of years there was nothing, wakening our awe. So much of what we give our best energies to, cultural, economic, political hierarchy, doesn't hold up so well in crunch time.

Paul Tsongas, the Massachusetts Senator, was diagnosed with leukemia. When he understood the likely outcome he resigned his seat. A friend asked him if it wasn't a big letdown giving up such an exalted position.

Paul smiled. "I don't remember anyone on their death bed saying, "I wish I'd spent more time at the office."

The meme on license plate holders: *Become the person your dog already thinks you are*, may be more than a cute idea.

Seminary Shaping

A bill to outlaw discrimination in public accommodations is languishing in the Senate, southern Democrats filibustering.

A student at the Jewish Theological Seminary in New York City sent a plea to seminarians across the country—Protestant, Roman Catholic, Jewish, Muslim—to come to Washington, stand vigil round the clock at the Lincoln Memorial until the bill is voted up or down.

I went with a group from Boston. We slept in sleeping bags on the floor of an Augustinian community in NE Washington, drawing from a hat, four-hour shifts. I drew a 4:00-8:00 A.M. shift on a bitter cold morning.

A rabbinical student picked up the Roman Catholic and me, drove us to the monument where we stood watch at a bench near the Memorial. He brought along a thermos of hot coffee.

We talked among ourselves about how our different traditions had come together to witness for racial justice. I was struck by how different the Roman Catholic's and my motivation was from the rabbinical student's.

The Roman Catholic and I were full of 1960s goodwill, for everyone. The Jew was pragmatic, hard-headed.

An American Nazi was standing counter-vigil at another bench, wearing Nazi military dress, and looked to be in his teens. Shivering in the pre-dawn cold.

The Roman Catholic said he was going to offer the boy hot coffee.

"Over my dead body," the Jew said. "Look, I'm under no illusion that this bill will end discrimination. But I know what can happen when the government comes down on the wrong side of a moral issue. I lost most of my family when that happened in Germany. All it takes to unleash the worst in people is for authority to sponsor it."

Hard truth: justice isn't merely about good people prevailing over bad people, but about making the cost of unleashing our dark side so costly it makes us reconsider.

It also prefigures the course of American politics in the ensuing years. We liberals seem still stuck in the place the Roman Catholic and I were in back then, dividing the world into good and bad people. Unlike the Rabbinical student who understood it isn't merely being reasonable that will address prejudice and violence. It's about doing all we can to call up our better angels and keep our dark angels from gaining the upper hand.

A hard reality: the social manners drilled into upper middle-class Americans like me lack the muscle required to right wrongs embedded in our national story. And in the dark side of each of us.

The young American Nazi went without hot coffee.

Playing For Keeps

Seminary and ordination, gaining insight and courage required for being Jesus' people, was turning out to be about a lot more than landing a job as pastor of a prosperous church. The church was finally becoming sensitive to ways her mission needs to be alert to cultural change. The struggle for racial justice in our culture meant having to set aside some of her institutional concerns. Like any change, this was hard, with plenty of resistance.

Sometimes called "the Republican Party at prayer," The Episcopal Church, entitled, seemingly appointed to dominate others, began to open herself to new realities that would alter her historic role.

The Episcopal Church was the only major denomination not split apart by the Civil War. Yes, obedience to Jesus outweighed obedience to ideology, but there was the practical consideration of not fracturing an already small communion.

The biggest rupture in our church's fabric in my time came when the Diocese of New Hampshire elected an openly gay, partnered man as their bishop. In a long, drawn-out, agonizing process, the American church, along with other churches in the worldwide Anglican communion, sought every imaginable compromise. They all failed. The American church affirmed ordination of gay people. An unusually principled moment of obedience to Jesus' mandate that, as the old hymn puts it, "In Christ there is no east or west, in Him not north or south, just one great fellowship of love . . ."

Significant numbers of Episcopalians left the American church and formed their own church under the jurisdiction of bishops from other countries, notably African and Latin American that condemned gay ordination and openly gay relationships.

Despite entertaining a host of prejudices, I'm grateful to have experienced God's grace, undeserved, unearned love, so powerful it can often overrule my persistent darker angels.

The Episcopal Church is hardly designed to wean us from middle-class prejudice. But for all her faults, the Episcopal Church owes her existence to Jesus. It doesn't take radical insight to understand that Jesus was not dedicated to preserving cultural power and privilege.

For those of us born to privilege, it can mean a plunge into uncharted waters: scary, thrilling, sometimes perilous, to find ourselves breasting unfamiliar currents.

Jon Daniels

First year seminary, theology seminar: each of us made a presentation. Since I arrived at seminary mostly ignorant of the discipline of theology, my presentation was a hit or miss (mostly miss) offering of 1960s feel-good.

The following week, Jon Daniels, classically trained in Thomistic thought, made a brilliant, dense offering, very different from mine.

Later a friend stopped me. "You must be pissed at Jon," he said.

"Why? Should I be?"

"Well, his paper was a wrecking ball aimed at yours of the previous week?"

I wasn't well enough schooled to have recognized that. I asked Jon why he used his time to attack my paper.

"It galls me," he said, "that you people with no training presume to make supposedly scholarly presentations."

Though I thought him high-handed, I knew he was right. It wouldn't be the last time I felt over my head trying to make language about God.

The next year John Lewis was nearly killed by Alabama State troopers crossing Pettus Bridge in Selma with a group protesting discrimination against Black voters.

Jon joined several hundred others from around the country to resume that march to Montgomery. Unlike most of the others, Jon stayed in Selma after the march. He lived with a family in the Black ghetto, tutored children, tried every Sunday, without success, to lead an integrated group to the local Episcopal Church.

He returned to Cambridge for his final exams. He and I ended up sitting on the dorm step on a warm spring afternoon. We rehearsed that incident from the previous year's theology class.

Jon apologized. "I was arrogant, insensitive."

"You were also right about my ignorance."

"You know, Blayney, if I've learned anything, living with that wonderful Black family in Selma, it is that recognizing the dignity of everyone, trumps so-called superior knowledge every time."

We talked for a couple of hours. Jon said he was going back to Selma for the summer.

"Jon, you're from New Hampshire. I grew up in the segregated south. The more moderate, mid-south. We knew better than to go to Alabama because those rednecks think nothing of shooting anyone they think is a threat to their way of life."

"I know that," Jon said. "Believe it or not, I've actually met a few White people in Selma who want to address racism.

"What's more, what my life has become since I went there, is so wonderful, so different from anything I've ever experienced. Even if I thought I might be killed, I'd go anyway."

Two months later on a Sunday morning, on the front page of the *New York Times* a story about Jon being shot to death in Alabama when he threw himself between a young Black girl and a White deputy sheriff with a shotgun.

All the theory about racism and violence took on flesh, Jon's bloody, murdered flesh. Jesus wasn't the last person executed for facing down unjust power. And Jon's murder wouldn't be the last time I felt over my head preaching love, refusing to bow to injustice. Ordination wasn't about being a respected member of society. It wasn't about encouraging people to adopt White, middle-class manners. It wasn't even about winning converts.

My breath caught in my throat as I read about Jon's murder. I excused myself from my friends with whom I was having breakfast. Went into the bathroom and sobbed. Sobbed for Jon's brutal death. And equally for the reality that Jesus was calling me to a life radically different from the life I had imagined. I realized it meant facing down a large part of me that hoped to be spared more than I thought I was capable of. Where to find that kind of courage? It's enough to drive a body to prayer. No wonder we clergy so often feed our congregations pap.

Nothing in me was eager for such a bold life. Yet Jon's martyrdom became another irreversible step toward the only choice that would scratch that persistent itch that had drawn me into seminary.

Dietrich Bonhoeffer, a brilliant young German, Lutheran pastor gassed by Nazis for being part of a plot to assassinate Hitler, wrote a book, *The Cost of Discipleship*. Like Jon, Bonhoeffer didn't shrink from what he knew he was being asked even when it cost him his life.

As a high-profile, Lutheran pastor he was sometimes among those called before Hitler. Hitler was determined to make the Lutheran Church the national ecclesiastical arm of the Nazis. In those meetings Bonhoeffer insisted on referring to Jesus as the Nazarene Rabbi. Always understanding the danger he was putting himself in.

What can persuade us of something so cardinal that not even fear of death will dissuade us?

Steadfast loyalty in the face of widespread opposition is how we have long portrayed those who were martyrs for Jesus; those who willingly faced death rather than make peace with oppression. As Jon did. As Bonhoeffer did.

Only very slowly did I begin to understand the Jesus standard calling me from my comfort zone.

My mother loved the comic strip *Pogo* in which Pogo says, "I have seen the enemy and he is us."

My naïve belief had been that it was a matter of suasion. Didn't we simply need to explain to people in power why sharing power, responding to calls for justice by those who have been denied, was not only the right thing to do, but the way we can get to the life we long for?

The facile cliché that the call of Jesus is to comfort the afflicted, and afflict the comfortable, can come too easily to a preacher's lips. Jon's murder made it clear it wasn't simple cliché. Or safe.

The Domination System

Walter Wink, a Methodist pastor and theologian, wrote that the central significance of Jesus' teaching, and what got him executed, was his refusal to be a part of what Wink called the Domination System.

The best way to understand this is to consider the people—women (in a male-dominated culture), tax collectors (hated for taking money from Jews to pay taxes to the Roman occupiers), simple, easily ignored fisher folk, a woman shunned for being divorced and living with a man to whom she wasn't married—all among Jesus' close companions. Even a Samaritan, ritually unclean to observant Jews, was a hero of a Jesus parable.

The first witness to Jesus' resurrection, the event Christianity holds as the center of its claim to God's revelation, was Mary Magdalene, therefore, likely with rightful claim as the first of Jesus' disciples. The male-dominated church still has a hard time acknowledging the preeminence of the least of these.

Getting My Feet Wet: Dying To Learn

Looking at those in my life who have had the deepest impact, it's surprising how many could be considered marginal when measured against those who are more honored. Maybe understandable since I see myself as marginal in so many ways.

Dick Trelease is the likely reason I managed to continue within the sometimes perplexing boundaries of priest and church, despite my restlessness with institutional life.

Nineteen-sixty-six: Fresh from seminary, and junior member of the staff of St. Paul's Church, Akron, Ohio. Sometimes teasingly called "St. Harvey's in-the-polo-field." (When the church moved from the decaying downtown to the prospering suburbs it was indeed built on Harvey Firestone's old polo field.)

What attracted me to ordained life, nearly as much as it terrified me, was knowing it would require me to belly up to death. Haunting memory of Jon Daniels.

My reluctance to embrace what was beyond reach of my overactive intellect. Everything about the American economy denies death, the great unmanageable unknown. It's as if that death may come for everyone else but never for me.

It didn't take long for my fear to be tested.

The day I showed up for work at St. Paul's, Akron, feeling as if my plastic clergy collar might choke me, I hadn't the faintest idea what that day, or the next many decades, might bring.

Dick Trelease, my new boss, met me at the door.

"I want you to go down to City Hospital to see Anabelle Tremere. She ran our Sunday School for twenty years. She's dying of lung cancer."

My heart raced. I felt light-headed. Dying? Really? "How do I get to City Hospital?"

He showed me a large map of the city pinned to the wall, pointed out a green X. "That's City Hospital. There's parking for clergy. Let me know how she's doing."

He disappeared into his office, closing the door.

I wrote down every turn I could make out on the map. I still made countless wrong turns, and it took me a half-hour to make the ten-minute trip, secretly hoping I might never get there.

I fumbled my way through parking, finding the reception desk, the right floor, awkwardly introduced myself to staff at the nursing station, and followed their directions to her room. There was Anabelle. Emaciated, shrunken cheeks, hospital bed cranked up to ease her labored breathing.

She greeted me with a big smile. "You're the new priest. How sweet of you to visit me."

I must have stayed an hour, way longer than one should. That she and I both smoked while we talked, reveals how long ago that was. Hospital room, woman dying of lung cancer, she and her priest casually smoking? Never gave it a thought.

I loved her.

"You must have a lot of other things to do today," she said, "I don't want to take up all your time."

I'd as soon have spent the rest of the day there. As I got up to go, she said, "I'm an old lady, dying because I've smoked most of my life. You're young, just getting started. You really should quit."

I smiled, thanked her. As soon as I got back in my car I lit another king-size Pall Mall.

I visited her many more times than pastoral responsibility would require. I never tired of our conversations.

One night the ringing phone woke me at 2 A.M. Anabelle's daughter.

"Mom's dying. They don't think she'll last the night."

I don't remember the rest of the conversation. I think I thanked her for calling, said goodbye, hung up, rolled over.

Maybe thirty seconds later, I sat straight up. Wait a minute, buddy, her mother's dying, she just called her priest. You're meant to go.

When I got to her hospital room, Anabelle was deep in coma, breathing erratically. Her daughter and son-in-law sat in chairs along the wall.

Smoking.

We greeted each other. I took a chair alongside them. Lit a cigarette. As Anabelle struggled for her next breath we filled the room with smoke.

Suddenly Anabelle opened her eyes wide, looked at me, and said, "Oh no, not yet!"

"Come hold me," she said.

I was frozen in place. Stood up, took a hesitant step towards her bed. Her eyes followed me.

"God damn it, hold me," she said, with startling energy in her voice.

I took a step closer, weaved my hands through the IV lines going into her body, put one hand beneath her back, one on her shoulder, pulled her gently toward me. She cried quietly.

Searching my memory for what I was supposed to do, say, I took my hand from behind her and made the sign of the cross on her forehead.

"Anabelle, unto God's gracious mercy and protection we commit you. The Lord bless you and keep you. The Lord make His face to shine upon you, and give you peace, for this day, and for your longest journey.

"Now go in peace to love and serve the Lord," I said, only later realizing that was the dismissal of the congregation when the service ends. It seemed right then. Still does.

Anabelle sighed. I let her back onto the pillow cautiously, making sure I didn't dislodge the IV lines. She closed her eyes. Maybe a faint smile? She seemed to sink into the bed. Sighed again. Her breathing shallow, faint.

Inhale. Totally still. No one spoke. Was I holding my breath, waiting for her next one? Just when it seemed certain she had taken her last breath, she took another. It rattled as if she needed to clear her throat.

Totally still. A few minutes? Nothing. The nurse came in, checked her pulse, left without saying anything.

The resident came, checked her again.

"She's gone," he said. Her daughter cried.

That simple? No trumpet, drum roll? One last inhale, no exhale. It's that easy?

The three of us stood, shifting awkwardly, unsure what to do next.

"Thank you for coming," her daughter said. We embraced. Her husband and I shook hands.

I walked out into the parking lot into the first light of dawn. Exhausted, I reached into my pocket for a cigarette.

"You dumb shit," I said to myself, "you just tended Anabelle's death. She died from smoking."

I crumpled up the package, tossed it into the wire basket. I'd had my last cigarette.

Thank you, Anabelle.

Politics and Religion

Early on I went to an organizational meeting of the Summit County Committee for Peace in Vietnam. I had come to consider our adventure there as using our superior power to dominate, dictate the terms on which another people and nations ought to live. Draining resources and attention from home: poverty, racism. Not to mention the lives of 58,000 young Americans.

Being the youngest, newest, greenest, least politically aware person at the meeting, I was elected president.

"You know you're going to be fired," one of the other clergy staff said, when he read of my election the next morning in the *Akron Beacon-Journal*.

"You think the power brokers in Rubber Gulch (as Akron was sometimes known then, still hosting the nation's biggest rubber producers) will stand for disrupting their lock on huge defense contracts?"

That hadn't occurred to me. I went to Dick Trelease, my boss, the rector, and offered to resign.

"Resign?!" he said, "We should nominate you for saint, for actually living Jesus' teaching."

That seemed a bit nobler than my motives in getting myself elected.

It etched a little deeper my sense that following Jesus' often perplexing teaching might actually have a practical agenda. Even in 20th century, power-obsessed USA.

And might not sit comfortably with church members whose power and wealth made big, wealthy churches like St. Paul's possible.

Dick stood before the congregation the Sunday I was in D.C. at the March on the Pentagon and praised me. Again suggested I was doing Jesus' work.

I later watched in awe as he led the vestry, the church lay governing body, in heated debate about whether to take a full-page ad in the *Beacon-Journal* in support of fair housing, calling on realtors to remove red-lines against Jews and Blacks buying houses in White neighborhoods.

He prevailed. At big cost. The head of the vestry, president of one of the rubber companies, vowed to make his life miserable for the rest of his tenure. Which he did.

Hidden in the anti-Vietnam War movement was an exorcism of western, White, male dominance that has haunted me since that morning my father knelt to commission me a budding patriarch. Though nothing weakens my intention to respect the integrity of what the Prayer Book calls "the least of these," my bones remain infected with White, western, male hierarchy.

Beloved and Flawed Mentor

What we believe, and how we act, aren't always in synch. Dick, whom I still hold in highest regard, turned out to be a flawed human. Like all of us.

Dick Trelease was my early model for how the power-post of rector (*rex, regis,* king) might be leveraged to challenge the power rich, privileged people hold over others.

A costly role, too easily mingled with ignoble urges. Ironically, as Dr. King's and John Lewis' rise to national prominence showed, being heard by power brokers seems to require gaining power.

Dick later became Bishop of the Rio Grande, a diocese made up of New Mexico and Southwest Texas. Huge in size but small in numbers of parishes. His car became his office as he traveled around the diocese.

Dick got together with a woman in one of his parishes. When the affair was discovered he resigned, disgraced.

I called to ask how he was managing. His voice was surprisingly upbeat.

"Selling men's shoes at a downtown department store," he said. "Everyone I work with has been wounded in some way. The kindest, most helpful colleagues I've ever worked with."

Curious that the disgraced bishop ended up embracing a piece of Jesus' teaching.

"Inasmuch as you have done it to one of the least of these," Jesus explained, "well, you have done it to me."

Sometime later Dick contacted me to say he intended to marry the woman. "The new bishop refuses to give me his permission. He said if I could find a bishop somewhere with such low morals as to agree to the marriage, he would not stand in his way."

"Dick," I said, "We're between bishops in San Diego. I'm head of the Standing Committee, which means I am the ecclesiastical authority. I'm sorry you wrecked your marriage, but I'm so glad you're willing to give marriage another go. Jesus refuses to give up on us. Come here and I'll officiate at your marriage."

They did. To be able to do that for Dick was a big thrill. They enjoyed several happy years together before Dick died. His widow asked me to preach at his funeral at the cathedral in Albuquerque.

Sermon Excerpt

"Did you know," Dick asked me one day, soon after he had hired me to be his curate in Akron, hoping to shake me loose from my parochial eastern Episcopal roots, "there are more Methodist churches in the State of Ohio than there are Episcopal churches in the entire United States?"

It would appeal to Dick's sense of irony, of God's stealth, that this Eucharist, in which we mark and celebrate his life, falls on the day our Church calendar remembers John and Charles Wesley, brothers, and Anglican priests whose passionate preaching of God's transforming love in the remote reaches of the southern frontier of colonial America became so powerful it could no longer be contained within the bounds of the Anglican Church, so it spilled, scandalously, into a new unseemly creation we now know as the Methodist Church.

What, one wonders, might it look like for Isaiah's promise of power, of a sumptuous feast, formed from bitter defeat, from the remnants of our broken lives, to leap from the dusty leaves of our Bible into the consuming heat of human flesh?

Maybe like the eighty-found years of the divine roller-coaster ride we have gone on with Richard Mitchell Trelease, Jr., whose brazen, living of God's overpowering love stirred our hunger for a taste of God beyond boundaries. Of God beyond God.

So this homily is about power and passion, gifts entrusted to us by God, for a season, and about Dick's lifelong, brave, sometimes reckless exercise of those gifts.

At first glance his passionate love of power looked to be for the usual reasons. Dick was a classy guy with classy appetites. The Akron parish gave the rector a new car every year, but in the interests of ecclesiastical modesty, insisted it be a Chevrolet. The vestry may never have known that Dick colluded with the local dealer, packing so much horsepower beneath the hood of that Chevy that he was finally driving a virtual Corvette in Caprice clothing. Clothes, rich food, well-aged wine, music, literature, success, professionally and in his personal dealings with people, Dick grabbed for the gold without apology and often grasped it.

But to understand Dick and his power, and passion, you must look at how he used it, and what it was like for him when, by the world's measure, he lost it.

When Dick Muir and I went to the March on Washington, the one best remembered for Norman Mailer's drunken call from the steps of the Pentagon for revolution, our brave boss again stood on the chancel steps and announced that we represented him and the whole staff.

Our enemies reveal as much about who we are as do our acolytes. Dick's enemies were, inevitably, those determined to manage the frightening embrace of God's transforming love on their own terms. Not that Dick, or any sane person welcomes the unmanageable encounter God's love always it, but those who trust God with the kind of daring Dick did, are in for a wondrous ride.

The bishop who succeeded Dick, a fussy English prig, found the sermon offensive, walked out as I preached. My uncharitable smugness at his taking offense made me realize I still had a long way to go before being able to practice my passion for justice without hating the oppressor.

If Not Now, When?

My first decade a priest, the issue of whether women would be ordained sparked a raging battle in the Episcopal Church. If it was good enough for Jesus, you might ask—considering Mary Magdalene—why such a wrench for the Episcopal Church? My surprise and chagrin was facing down my discomfort with the possibility.

Guarding my prerogatives? Threatened by strong women? Afraid of change?

All of that. While grasping the justice and good sense of women priests, its chipping away at centuries of male domination, I nonetheless balked. Maybe, despite my discomfort inhabiting male hierarchy ever since my father anointed me, it was familiar. Seemed built-in. I chided myself for my complicity. For my resistance to change.

I hearkened back to a friend who had harbored a deep dislike for '60s radicals, hippies. Their facial hair, symbol of their caste, offended his sense of decorum.

He decided the way to face down own prejudice was to emulate those for whom he had contempt. He grew a handlebar mustache.

"Did it help?" I asked him.

"Only after several months, when I began to really like it. Especially when my buttoned-down friends asked me when I was going to shave the wretched thing off."

He went to his grave fully hirsute, his final decades in solidarity with those he once disdained.

From that seemingly simple gesture I learned something about my embarrassingly entrenched blindness: the best way to face prejudice in people who threaten you, is to throw in your lot with them. Maybe still some way to go to be able to embrace Jesus' command to love our enemies.

I was less in tune with my second boss who I thought was preoccupied with maintaining his place in the city hierarchy. He focused on proper dress and manner, aping those he envied. And he meant to impose those standards on those of us who worked for him.

No loafers, only tie shoes. Never cross your legs while in the chancel during worship. No eye contact with worshippers from the chancel. Hair never below shirt collar. If a vestry member invited me to dinner, I was to consult him before accepting.

I habitually chafe under arbitrary authority. First year in that job, while on vacation, I grew a handlebar mustache. When I returned, my boss simply noted my new growth. A couple of weeks later he told me he thought I was ready to move on.

I agreed, though it took me a hellish long time to find a new job. He and I managed a polite standoff during that interim.

None of us is beyond being seduced by power.

Watergate
Nixon's Enemies List

Wanting to be accepted into the same hierarchy I was determined to eschew, crept into my behavior in ways that can still make me squirm.

St. John's, Lafayette Square, in Washington, D.C., is known as The Church of the Presidents. Every President since Monroe has worshipped there (most rarely, simply keeping alive the tradition of going there the morning of their inauguration.) I had an office that looked over Lafayette Park to the White House.

I found that seductive, thrilling. That I did, now embarrasses me.

I discovered in a curious way how unprepared I was for the strange world of Washington.

The year before I moved there, I went on the infamous anti-Vietnam War March on the Pentagon. Harking back to my civics classes in representative democracy, I wrote a letter to the President explaining that I was coming on the march to support what I was sure was his wish to end the war.

I received a reply. From the Assistant Attorney General, on Justice Department stationery.

"Dear Rev. Colmore, The President has received your letter and asked me to take note of your views . . ."

Naïve as I then was, I didn't grasp the significance of the reply, not from the White House, nor the Defense Department, but from the agency that deals with criminal behavior.

A few months after I began at St. John's, Daniel Schoor, Washington correspondent for *ABC News*, held a press conference one day in St. John's parish house to cover a demonstration in Lafayette Square.

I introduced myself to Schoor. When I said my name he looked at me curiously. "Blayney Colmore . . . why is your name familiar to me?"

I had no idea.

"I know why," he said, his eyes widening, "Did you know you're on Nixon's enemies list?"

My surprise and dismay must have been all over my face.

Schoor laughed. "I wouldn't get too puffed up about it. It's a long list, and you're nowhere near the top where people like me are, who they intend to harass."

Decades later, reading still more about those times, I learned that someone in the White House had leaked a copy of the enemies list, updated daily as Nixon's opposition grew, to Schoor the night before, and he'd stayed up late that night, after finding his own name, with a threatening marginal note about needing to take him down.

Imagine the diligence of some staff member unearthing the name of an obscure priest who had been on that march and was now the junior member of the staff at the church across the park from the White House.

Access Dilutes Principle

I was 29 years old when I began at St. John's, the age of many of the White House staff. The 24-hour demands of White Hose staff are unsustainable for anyone much older.

I became friends with a few of them, notably Jeb Magruder.

Though I didn't make a big thing of it, my friends in the White House knew I was a Democrat who opposed the war, who regarded their Southern Strategy, appealing to southern racists that likely won them the election, abhorrent.

You'll know how long ago (1970) that was by the fact that, instead of harboring animosity about our differences, we teased each other.

From time to time I had lunch in the West Wing White House mess, and played tennis with Jeb on the White House court.

One day after tennis I was getting dressed in the gym dressing room in the White House basement. Dwight Chapin, Nixon's appointment secretary, walked by as I snapped on my clergy collar. "Jesus, Jeb," he said, "has it come to this; that we need to play tennis with the clergy to get God on our side?"

Jeb was in charge of Inauguration ceremonies at the start of Nixon's second term. My wife and I were invited to an inaugural ball, and to sit in the stands for the parade on Pennsylvania Avenue.

You might wonder why an unrepentant Democrat would cozy up to an administration that gained its power appealing to what I considered our worst instincts.

It's a question I still ask myself. The answer, that was eventually provided by Jeb, still makes me squirm.

Watergate was heating up but I had no idea of its breadth and complexity until one night at a going-away party for us, as we were moving to Dedham.

Jeb whispered in my ear that he needed to talk. We went into a bedroom and closed the door.

"I spent the day at the prosecutor's office," he said. "I turned state's evidence, told them everything."

Stunned, I asked, "What's everything, Jeb?"

"That we've been lying about this Watergate thing the whole time. A lot of people will be going to jail, and I'm one of them."

Fast forward something over a year. Jeb has done a seven-month term in Danbury prison. He came to stay with us in Dedham shortly after being released, as he licked his wounds, went through a divorce.

A group of parishioners learned he was staying with us, asked if he might be willing to talk with them. I knew most were Republicans (albeit, of a liberal, Yankee stripe that today would be unrecognizable as Republicans). Jeb was a clean-cut young guy who would fit comfortably into Dedham.

Before the meeting he warned me of a question he knew someone would ask, and ran the answer by me to see if I could live with it. I said I could.

Sure enough: "Jeb, you're a seemingly reasonable guy, good education, good ethics, how did you ever let yourself get in that mess?"

Jeb smiled. "Do you think your rector has integrity?" he asked.

"Of course," the questioner said.

"So do I," Jeb said. "We all knew he didn't think much of our administration but I don't remember his ever turning down lunch in the White House Mess or tennis on the White House Court.

"Until you've experienced being around that kind of power it's impossible to understand its seductive power."

Everyone in the room looked at me. I tried to make light of it.

"The food was good, and I always beat Jeb at tennis," I said. It drew a laugh, but I knew it wasn't funny. Yes, what Jeb said is right. It embarrasses me now to face how much I let what I thought was bedrock for me, be compromised by the seduction of access to power.

It also explains how glad I was to leave Washington, where the power game pretty much eclipsed everything.

Even now I wonder if I would be strong enough to withstand its pull. Did I retire early, not only because I wanted to write, but also because I'm not strong enough to eschew the perks and privilege that are visited on rectors of powerful Episcopal Churches?

It was a relief to finally move from D.C. I am chagrined to admit that the sophisticated seduction of the power elite made me wonder how strong my resolve was to live out my connection to "the least of these."

Why Not Ordained Women?

My discomfort with women being admitted to the hierarchy of ordination was akin to White people's uneasiness with Black people taking their rightful place in the ranks of leadership.

What would it be like to submit to the authority of a woman bishop? Be treated by a Black doctor? Experiences I've had in ensuing years, that have enlarged my world, but still haven't entirely expunged my bones of prejudice.

The issue is change. The Episcopal Church, heir to the Church of England, in business since the 16th century: No women clergy.

I knew my reluctance was ill-founded, simple prejudice. A matter of justice, not to mention recognizing the unique gifts of women, so suitable to pastoral ministry.

But the opposition, like all opposition based on unexamined prejudice, was fierce.

Taking another page from my friend who risked facial hair to dent his prejudice, I hired a woman seminarian who was in the militant forefront of the fight for ordaining women. Pattie considered it great sport to challenge my clinging to male prerogatives, especially those I was unaware of. Which were legion. Parishioners found her overly aggressive, confronting. Several asked me to fire her. I admired her courage, even though the way she disrupted life in the parish unnerved me, calling from me more unrecognized, embarrassing efforts to smooth over conflict rather than face its cause.

A few years later, more than twenty years ordained, rector of a second, much larger parish, the first ordained women finally emerging into full life in the church, I hired a woman associate, the first woman in the Diocese of San Diego, to be a parish pastor.

The retired bishop of the diocese, and one-time rector of the parish where I was now rector, had led opposition to women's ordination in the House of Bishops. He worshipped at his/our parish. Despite our many differences, he had been warmly welcoming to me.

I called on him to tell him of my decision to hire Susan. He listened, reminded me of his long opposition to women priests. Then: "You're the rector, Blayney, you have to make these decisions." I thanked him for listening, and left, wondering how he might react.

"You know the bishop will leave the parish," someone warned me, "and likely take his considerable following with him."

He stayed, showing up weekly for the lightly attended 7:30 A.M. service.

He always chose to receive communion at whichever side of the rail was being administered by a male priest.

Until the day I saw him cross to the side Susan was tending.

"Did you see the bishop take communion from me?" Susan asked after the service.

I waited a few weeks, watched him receive at seemingly random sides, including Susan's, before saying anything to him.

"Bishop," I said, "I really appreciated you sticking around after I hired Susan. I know it wasn't easy. And I especially admire you receiving communion from her. I can only imagine what that took."

He regarded me silently with a solemn expression. "I was wrong about ordaining women," he said. "It took me a long time to admit it, but now I can see how much they have added to the life of the church."

Like my friend who grew a mustache, the bishop showed me how a person can keep growing, even in old age.

Yes, alas, I considered myself a liberal hero, a sign that I still too easily fell into an old trap, thinking male power had made that change possible.

Eventually each of those two women faced me down about my self-congratulation and confronted me with my habitual wobbling.

Pattie took me to task for supporting the abusive husband of an alcoholic woman, pointing out that my discomfort with her addiction didn't excuse her husband's abuse.

She helped me understand addiction as a hard, human issue that limits lives, rather than something to hold in contempt or consider susceptible to my gentle pastoral suasion. Thanks to Pattie's intervention, with me, and with the woman, the woman not only got sober, but became a leader in AA, invaluable in helping others with addiction.

A couple of years later, she gave me a needed tutorial in working with alcoholics.

"When someone comes to talk to you about their drinking, listen, but don't try to offer counsel. Or sympathy. Give them my name, or the name of another member of AA. Your natural compassion, and discomfort with confrontation will let them run circles around you and keep them from facing reality. You're not a drunk. You don't get it."

Her wise counsel saved me from perpetuating my destructive tendency to believe my compassion and insights were enough to wean people from addiction.

In Susan's case, I had hired her as associate rector, after hiring another, male, associate. Not having anticipated hiring a second priest, the budget had been set. There wasn't money to pay them equally.

Did I tell her that I wasn't able to offer her the same salary as the man I'd hired? That we intended to set it right in the next year's budget? My memory that I had, turned out to be wrong, self-serving my conscience.

After a meeting at which clergy salaries were among discussed subjects, she called me, irate.

"You son-of-a-bitch! You thought you were a wonderful liberal, hiring a woman. Then you sabotaged me the way women have been sabotaged forever, paying me less for the same job as the man. Set it right or I'll quit, expose you for the hypocrite you are."

We set it right. Didn't wait for the next year. It meant throwing the budget into deficit. She went on to be a valued, beloved priest at that parish, a valuable colleague, and later rector of her own parish. Her charisma attracted more support than it cost the budget.

After lunch one day with Bishop Katharine, former Presiding Bishop of the USA, I came away with a different sense than any I'd had over the years in several encounters, with men bishops.

Being with her was more like being with a compassionate friend, not a member of a hierarchy, as I usually experienced with male bishops.

Her unmistakable authority was herself, not her position. A revelatory moment.

The Character of Justice

Bryan Stevenson, founder of Equal Justice Initiative, and the Lynching Museum in Montgomery, Alabama, has said, "The opposite of poverty isn't wealth. The opposite of poverty is justice."

A retired colleague and I were led on a pilgrimage by Jo, another retired colleague who had been raised in the region of several historic civil rights sites in Alabama, including Hayneville, where Jon Daniels had been murdered.

He teased us about being Yankee liberals with little understanding of rural southern culture. "I'm going to make you two into rednecks before this visit is over," he teased. During the course of that trip we discovered that Jo, like a lot of White people immersed in the deep south who didn't cotton to the contempt many White people had for Black people, was formed in ways nearly incomprehensible to his two friends.

At a library in Jo's hometown, Livingston, Alabama, named for his aunt who had provided funding to build it, a meeting was just breaking up, led by an African-American general who emerged from the meeting room in full dress uniform.

Jo immediately engaged him in military talk—Jo had put in time in the Marines—and it developed that Jo and the general had grown up within a few miles of each other. They embraced as they exchanged stories about what it was like to grow up White in Livingston, and what it was like to grow up Black.

And how glad they were that old barriers were starting to fall.

Our other colleague/friend and I watched with fascination as the two men seemed to transcend boundaries in some way the two of us knew only in theory. As we talked about it later we admitted we would have been uncomfortable in that exchange. We confirmed Jo's telling us there's no substitute for having experienced close intimacy with poor and Black people in the rural south, even though it's history is so fraught with injustice.

I got a keener sense of why racial justice seems so elusive. Black and poor White people have been in a separate world from those of us who have lived in middle-class White enclaves. We don't know each other well enough to trust each other.

We spent several hours in the National Memorial for Peace and Justice, the Lynching Museum, in Montgomery. The voices and artifacts of those

American martyrs need to be heard by all of us. It was a sobering experience.

People, almost all Black men, jailed for all manner of reasons, some justified, many not, were interviewed, filmed in their prison cells. We read about our nation having the highest per capita rate of incarceration in the world. Seeing—listening to—people describe their experience, put discomforting flesh on the previously bare bones of reading about them.

What might justice look like in our culture, long distinguished by rewarding wealth and power? Our national energies spent reinforcing hierarchy, power, even when it requires violence. Harsh injustice. Contrary to our national boast about the land of equal opportunity.

My adult life is been at least partially spent meaning to unlearn the lessons of preserving my own prerogatives, prerogatives that once seemed my birthright.

Lifelong Learning

Walking through Boston Common one damp, cold afternoon—now ten years ordained, rector of St. Paul's. Dedham, Massachusetts—with John, a clergy colleague. Large bodied, red-faced, ill-fitting, shiny, black suit, high, stiff clerical collar, John was a priest from a different tradition from mine. More kin to Roman Catholic spiritual formation than the old-boy world I knew.

I was the old Yankee-type clergy. Khaki pants, tweed sport coat, button down shirt, rep tie. Who would have picked me off as priest?

A disheveled, man of indiscriminate age, staggered toward us.

"All yours," I said to my colleague, knowing the man had spotted his clerical collar.

"Hey Father," he mumbled, "spare a few bucks for me to get something to eat?"

John smiled warmly. "I guess I could spring for that," he said, and reached into his pocket, pulled out a $5 bill which he handed to the man.

"May God be merciful to you, Dear Man," John said as the man thanked him and walked away.

I laughed. "You think he's going to spend that money on food?" I asked, smugly. "He'll head straight for the liquor store."

"Maybe he needs a drink worse than he needs food," he said.

John's merciful justice shredded another piece of my conditioning to measure people's worth by their place in the hierarchy. By whether their appearance and manner confirm my prejudices about who belongs. Who counts.

"Who knows?" John said, drilling into me a lesson I was loathe to learn, "he may have been Jesus, come to offer us a chance to be a part of his mercy."

Vexing, the distance between what I know is right, and the irrational feelings (fear?) that can stand between my convictions and my actions.

Humbling Reality

I became rector of Dedham at 32, long before I understood much of anything about anything. I had become skilled at the tasks of rector, preaching, pastoral care, but hadn't absorbed the purpose underlying those skills.

Nor had I grown mature enough to keep from being drawn into the wayward habits of our '60s generation. More authority than we were ready for. One year *Time Magazine* named 30-year-olds "Person of the Year." We believed we were taking over, and the world would be glad we were.

My marriage was shaky, at least in part because I thought my restlessness was due to having made a poor marriage choice. I didn't feel fulfilled.

All around us couples our age were getting divorced. My wife and I made that disruptive decision, no doubt thinking we were making a brave choice for richer life. As I look back, with no little sorrow, I see that we considered the effort required to probe whether we might have built a future together, the patience and discipline required, was greater than we were willing to take on.

What about our vows? Our three young children?

All these years later I still sorrow over my failing to wrestle harder with that. Who knows whether our decision may have been best for us, but we followed the trend at the time, hardly acknowledging the gravity of what we were doing. Years later, the hard work of knitting a step-family into some semblance of a healthy entity, cured us of any remaining smugness.

Two years later, by God's grace, I fell in love with Lacey, also recently divorced with two children, and after a courtship—tricky for rector of a parish in a tight community—we married.

Though that has turned out to be among the most fortuitous pieces of my life, I went into that marriage with no more sense of what it was about, than I had the first time.

Lucky for me Lacey was more grown up. Her first lesson for me was understanding her fierce determination.

Strong incentive to remain faithful.

When her first marriage dissolved, Lacey made a pledge to herself that she would do whatever needed for her two young children not to suffer deficits from something they didn't choose. Of course, they had their share of hard knocks, but it wasn't for lack of her unflagging effort.

One evening as dinner was being readied, I walked by two-year-old Oakley who was sitting in a highchair. Lacey had put carrot slices on the tray in front of him to keep him occupied as she cooked.

I casually picked up a slice as I passed him, popped it into my mouth. He set up an ear-piercing wail. Lacey rushed over, wondering if she was going to see blood.

"What's wrong?" she asked him.

"Blayney took one of my carrots."

Lacey motioned me out of the room.

"Don't you ever do anything like that again. Do you understand me? Never help yourself to their food."

It was an early lesson, not only in her maternal determination that would brook no carelessness from me, but in her willingness to go to the mat for what mattered to her, even when it created friction between us.

Those were the days of young couples experimenting with sexual relationships beyond marriage. When someone asked Lacey whether she worried about me doing that, she said, "No. He's free to do whatever he wants, so long as he's willing to risk having his balls shot off."

I wasn't.

The very conventional parish had never experienced a divorced rector. Since, the Episcopal Church had only recently made it possible for divorced clergy to remain in their post (bowing to cultural reality, as divorce became common among clergy), nor had many parishes.

They were generous with me, the parish leaders working hard with the bishop to keep the lid on. But there was growing uneasiness with my position as rector.

Lessons From
the African Bush

Having been rector for ten years, the vestry gave me a sabbatical. After much debate, Lacey and I fell under the spell of our bishop, John Coburn, who had just returned from a visit to Zimbabwe.

As he described his time there it was as if he was inviting us into an experience of another dimension. He was a measured man, not given to displaying emotion, but when he talked about encountering African spirituality he could have passed for born-again.

We were up for an adventure we thought we understood. I have heard Africa described as the place where all western, rational answers are turned back into questions. Good description of our time there.

We started our time in Africa as countless Americans have, arrogant in estimating our courage, ignorant in acknowledging our limits. We'd told Bishop Jonathon

Siyachitema we were ready for a rural experience. He assigned us to the Diocesan school deep in the bush. It had been badly damaged by their recent bloody war against the Ian Smith regime.

The house they'd worked so hard to arrange for us had no hot water. Rumor had it that even the trickle of water from the spigot was from the polluted nearby river.

As we unpacked we stepped into a nest of fire ants that stung us up and down our legs. When Lacey went to use the nearby loo, the tiny room was crawling with big spiders and iguanas. Louise and Oakley happily arranged their few stuffed animals on their cots and quickly fell asleep.

Lacey and I entered into a tense exchange about whether we were safe. We were two hours from the nearest medical facility, hard driving through dense bush.

The next morning we bailed. Embarrassed, humbled, we made some lame excuse to the bishop. After letting us sit with our humiliation for a spell, the bishop, announced, as if from a vision, "This isn't the place God intended for you."

He fleshed out his holy insight, calling his Archdeacon about a vacant post deep in the rural southernmost part of the country where sugar cane growing had attracted White managers and African workers.

We were pretty clear from the outset that we had a hard time with the sharp division between Black and

White Africans. And with the living conditions of the cane workers that were so reminiscent of the segregated south where I grew up.

The White Africans (all subsumed under the name "Europeans") were pretty clear we were typical American liberals who understood nothing about the relationships we were judging.

They were right about us. The proof of the ambiguity, and our piece of it, was that we came to cherish friendships with a handful of Europeans. Friendships that endure to this day. We've had no enduring connection to Black Africans.

The unofficial apartheid was reflected in the small Parish of Apollos the Irrigator.

The parish was in the Lowveld, an arid region in which Mauritians had built channels from a dam up north, bringing water to irrigate the sugar, the staple of the region. Thus, the parish—St. Apollos, the Irrigator. (1 Corinthians 3: 6. "I, Paul, planted, Apollos watered, and God gave the growth.")

Sunday morning, we rose early for a 7 A.M. Eucharist at the tiny church building next to the house we lived in. Almost exclusively a White congregation.

Then packed up the Communion vessels and drove 20 miles to Triangle, another sugar cane producing community, where the congregation was mixed, with many "colored" (meaning mixed race), some Black Africans, a few Europeans.

From there we went to the small stone church in Tshovani, the African township where the congregation was all Black and the most responsive and joyful of the three. It was midday by then, the temperature risen into the 90s and the church an oven.

Booker, the Black catechist of the multi-racial, radically stratified congregations that made up the parish, was pastor in every way except the privileges visited on me by ordination.

In the Tshovani church I celebrated Eucharist in halting Shona, reading from the Prayer Book, preaching in English while Booker translated. I looked to him to direct me multiple times as I lost my way.

I wore short pants beneath my white cassock, because of the stifling heat. Adult Whites wore shorts. Africans considered them proper only for children. Once, illustrating something in the sermon, I pulled open my cassock, revealing my shorts. Booker went silent. I asked him, "Aren't you going to translate, Booker?" "No, Baba, not that one." Only later did I understand he was trying to save me the humiliation a grown man in shorts would suffer in Shona culture.

Booker, Gentle Teacher

He came to me one morning with news that a young woman with no husband and two small children had died of malaria. He explained that I was to come to a place where her body would be, do her funeral (in Shona), take a ceremonial part in preparing her body to be placed in a lorry to be transported the long distance to her tribal land where she would be buried.

Booker knew I was flying blind, unfamiliar with all that went into such a moment. He generously treated me as if I was conversant with all that was to go on, quietly directing my every move, whispering in my ear what I must do next.

The men built a wood casket to carry her body only to discover the casket that fit her body was too long to fit into the lorry that would take her body back to her homeland for burial. They summoned me (and Booker) to come into the shed where they were working and described their dilemma. Booker carried on an animated exchange with them about what the solution might be.

He whispered to me that I was being asked to grant them absolution to break her legs so she could be fit into a shorter casket the lorry could hold. Before they would do that they wanted reassurance they would not be judged uncaring, sinful.

I swallowed hard, my discomfort causing me to nearly wretch, while praying for her and for the men, making the absolving sign of the cross, only allowed, in their eyes, to a priest. And watched while they broke her legs.

They brought her out from the shed, her body in the casket, her legs covered with a blanket. When the lorry pulled away, to a loud chorus of ululating from her women friends, I gave a final blessing.

On the ride home, Booker praised me for having done a masterful job under difficult circumstances. He would hear nothing of my insisting that it was he, not me, who had orchestrated it all.

Later, deeply shaken, I reflected on the soldiers at Jesus' crucifixion, breaking his legs before removing his body from the cross to hasten his dying so he could be buried before sundown. It did nothing to lessen how deeply I was shaken, but it did a lot to teach me about the terrible, fleshy solemnity that western Christianity finds too close to the bone. And to appreciate in new ways, that my job was to offer myself for much that unnerved me and could hardly bear.

Not to mention the dignity of the likes of Booker, who bore authentic marks of Jesus.

Later, when the time for us to return from sabbatical was nearing, Bishop Siyachtema, the Shona prelate to whom I reported, asked me not to leave. There was no priest to succeed me. I explained I was obligated to return to the parish that was paying my salary while I was in Zimbabwe.

The notion of money overriding the need for a priest was unfathomable to the bishop.

"I hear there are so many priests in America, some are pumping petrol because there is no need for them in churches." (Slight exaggeration, but not altogether untrue.)

"Bishop," I said, "why not ordain Booker? He would make a wonderful pastor for this parish."

Bishop Syichatema looked at me as if I had broken wind. "Booker has never even been to England," he said.

The Black majority had won the bloody war for their independence from England only eight years earlier. But the African Anglicans, all of whom had received their theological education in England, prized that credential, despite all it said about discounting the blood shed for African autonomy and against despised colonialism. And dignity.

I learned more about the mysteries of Jesus from Africans than I did in three years of seminary. Had it not been for those sublime, overturning months in remote, rural Zimbabwe, confounded most every day,

I don't know that our marriage or my vocation would have survived.

I had to die to nearly everything I thought I understood and believed. Including what I brought to a marriage. And to being priest. Every self-confident American would do well to have a spell in Africa.

Whatever self-righteousness remained to me about how to combat racism, inequality, injustice, evaporated. Americans learned colonialism from the Europeans. We now have our own colonial history.

I left Africa as deeply troubled as ever by all of that. A surprising amount of Africans' ways of following Jesus had seeped into even my skeptical, cerebral, habits, in ways I couldn't have imagined.

As I reflect, I understand Carl Jung having been profoundly impacted by Africa where he spent even less time than I did. North American spirituality can leave the deeper, non-cognitive, bodily dimension untouched. Jung's work on the unconscious, whether specifically Christian or not, seems more open to the radical changes (metanoia) Jesus asks of us, than merely subscribing to a set of ideas and doctrines.

I was already too old (44) to be totally cleansed of wanting to "understand" before giving myself. But every member of our family will tell you Africa marked all our lives in ways that, nearly forty years later, endure.

Can't Go Home Again

When we agreed to the sabbatical Bishop Coburn had called to congratulate me.

"Congratulate me?" I asked, "Who wouldn't jump at a chance for a many-month respite from normal duties?"

"Just about anyone, considering what's involved," he said. "You'll be gone long enough to change, see new ways of doing and being. Your parishioners won't have had those experiences. What's more, it's long enough for them to realize they can get along without you. And it often happens that they'll begin to want to do just that."

I hadn't considered all that. It wasn't long before I began to understand the bishop's insight.

We returned to Yankee Dedham, filled with new spirit, and soon discovered Dedham was perfectly happy with her own spirit that she had evolved over many generations. The parish was kind, generous, and, increasingly less subtle, anxious for me to find a parish that was more eager for whatever we thought we were bringing from Zimbabwe. And not have to confront the discomfort of a divorced rector and step-family.

I imagined people, seeing us coming, said, "Here come the Colmores, don't mention Africa or we'll be here all afternoon."

Working-class English

From this safe vantage point, I see many things about Dedham that were a little too challenging to have considered when I was rector.

When George Floyd's murder super-charged the Black Lives Matter movement, some things about the suburban, lily-White parish sprang to mind.

Dedham was begun in 1635, as a Land Grant from the British Crown. Over ensuing centuries—after a struggle over whether they would be loyal to the Crown, or finally join the Revolution, which they did, it took on the character of an English village, pieces of which remain in curious ways.

When Dedham took the side of the Revolution, St. Paul's rector, who'd sworn allegiance to the Crown, was driven into exile, and died on a boat moored off the coast.

Dedham is divided by Route 1, a major artery from Boston leading to the western suburbs.

One side of Route 1 looks for all the world like a prosperous town you might find outside London. It has long been known as Precinct One. Landed gentry have inhabited Precinct One for nearly four-hundred years. St. Paul's parish, also established by a Land Grant, still holds 999-year leases to some of the prized land in the Precinct.

A comical (maybe not so funny?) annual occurrence was the vestry meeting at which we would consider a petition from someone buying a house and discovering they couldn't get clear title to the land, because the land belonged to St. Paul's. Rent the church was entitled to collect (and not paid for at least a century) was mostly in kind: a sheaf of wheat (no longer grown in Dedham).

Younger members of the vestry, considering this archaic arrangement silly (and imagining being in the position of the buyer), argued for selling the land lease and cleaning up the church's balance sheet.

One of the older members would always veto that suggestion. "That land is valuable. We should wait until the lease expires (at that point another 800 or so years) when the church will be in a powerful bargaining position."

The half of Dedham on other side of Route 1 was settled by English working-class who served the people in Precinct One.

St. Paul's early parishioners felt their servants ought to have a church. But unthinkable that they would worship with their "betters." So they founded (and funded) The Church of the Good Shepherd. Still today its building, appointments, Communion silver (more modest), and, scandalously, the rector's salary subsidized by the Diocese, is considerably lower than that of St. Paul's rector.

The two parishes shared a few common moments through the year, notably each parish ceasing its main service while the rector takes vacations: one in July and one in August. We always piously claimed this was how we would get to know each other and begin to break down the class distinctions that still haunt our country today.

This vacation schedule ignored the reality that virtually all of Precinct One was away in their vacation homes on Cape Cod, and/or coastal Maine, during those two months. July, when Good Shepherd closed, St. Paul's normally moribund summer attendance, grew. August, when St. Paul's closed, Good Shepherd's attendance hardly changed.

One day, during the annual softball game between the two churches, the class tensions came to a head. St. Paul's curate (assistant priest), a hard-charger by instinct, hit a single. Then, violating whatever propriety there may have been, he stole second base. Good Shepherd's catcher fired a perfect strike to the second baseman. He leaned down to tag out the curate, who slid in, spikes high, and drew blood from the second baseman.

Both benches emptied, a brawl ensued, luckily, stopped by cooler heads on both sides.

Centuries of animosity had found its expression. And we faced the awful reality of prejudice between Episcopalians of different means that erased any common allegiance to Jesus.

After that we had an annual picnic, sparsely attended. No more softball.

Class, economic prejudice, as pervasive as racial prejudice, and, as we're experiencing now, every bit as threatening to the American experiment in being able to self-govern an increasingly diverse nation.

LaLa Land

Fourteen years, divorce and new marriage, a life-changing sabbatical in Zimbabwe, the tensions from staying at St. Paul's for what I now consider too long, led me to accelerate my search for a new post. Not easy for a divorced and remarried priest.

That led us, surprisingly and happily to southern California, and a culture and piety quite different from Yankee sensibilities. Maybe less suspicious of trusting intuition? That's what makes people in the east consider California the land of flakes. I've never totally connected with southern California culture either, but find it fascinating, challenging. And, after the more austere, Yankee culture, quite fun.

If I can't yet forgive myself for not having character enough to resist power's temptations in D.C., I can only barely admit how much living by the Pacific Ocean, swimming through the winter, seemed as profoundly an experience of God's grace as anything I've read in the Bible or experienced in church.

Those were fascinating nine years. I told New England friends that La Jolla was, in ways that snuck up on me, more like Zimbabwe had been, than like the Yankee world where I'd spent that past several decades.

Though the congregation was mostly Anglo, the proximity to Mexico influenced the culture more than those Anglos were aware or might admit. The prejudices I experienced growing up in Charlotte, and, more subtly everywhere else, in southern California are focused more on Mexicans, who are neighbors as close as the South Carolina border was to Charlotte.

On any given Sunday, in the congregation of a couple of hundred people, probably nearly half had been raised Roman Catholic. The parish was a combination of divorced people, who could not receive communion in the Roman Catholic Church, and those who rebelled against their strict parochial upbringing. They often found the Elizabethan remnants in Episcopal worship, more satisfying than the vernacular liturgy the Roman Catholic Church which evolved after Vatican II.

The Episcopal Church is often teased as being "Catholic-lite."

It was my first experience of the more ceremonial, sacramental "high Church." At first, I found it discomforting. Probably the prejudice against Irish Catholics that pervaded Yankee culture, and my upbringing, caused me to chafe under it.

Had it not been for the Zimbabwe sabbatical, where unapologetic spiritualism, accented with animism,

I doubt I could have let La Jolla's Latin sensibilities reshape my experience of church and God, as it did.

Even so, it took a while.

Preparing for my first Eucharist, I went into the vesting sacristy and found a full set of vestments laid out for me. I confessed to the altar-guild lady on duty that I had never worn them. She looked incredulous.

"Just stand still," she said, "I'll dress you."

She did.

A Eucharist every day of the year, often two. Sacramental confession and saints days were all new to me. To my surprise I came to deeply appreciate that tradition. It made sense of the role of priest in ways the less defined, rational, Yankee, role of minister in the more Protestant tradition, never had. Another expression of how Africa had impacted my sensibility.

Those years etched in me a deeper sense of the mystery of ordination and, at the same time, prepared me to step away from the institutional role that led people to assume I had mystical powers. I came to see that ordination—offering one's self for people's mystical (even, sometimes, magical) projections—is built into the priestly role. It wasn't about something that ordination added to my bag of tricks, but an identity, a job description that includes accepting projections people cast onto those in arcane roles.

In many ways Priest is the western version of Shaman. Both as healer, soothsayer, medium, conduit to a dimension we all know is out there, but find frustratingly elusive to rational, linear mind.

Grateful for those rich years, I see church and priest, as having provided me with a way to be of use, to inhabit sacraments that dance around that murky line between ordinary time and whatever may lie in wait for us beyond. Aging has eroded my suspicion of the non-linear dimension, but I continue to wonder.

The writing I've been doing in the ensuing years has been another chapter in my searching for ways to invite readers (and myself) into trusting that elusive "other" we somehow know waits our attention.

Sister Electa

California introduced me to spiritual direction. I'd done a fair amount of therapy, but not this. Thanks to colleagues, I found my way to Sister Electa, a Discalced (shoeless) Carmelite, who had been in enclosure longer than I'd been alive.

Electa, 4'10," bent to the right at an 80° angle from multiple back surgeries, on a crutch, with one built-up shoe. Maybe the most physically challenged person I'd ever known who was still upright. And the most cheerful, affirming person I've ever encountered.

When you walked into the monastery, it was eerily quiet, seemingly deserted. Straight ahead, a dumb waiter with a sign saying, "Ring bell." When you did, a disembodied voice asked, "May I help you?"

"I'm here to see Sister Electa."

The dumb waiter turned. On the opening was a key.

"It's the key to Speak Room Number 3," the voice said. "Down the hall on the left."

You walked down, unlocked the door to Speak Room Number 3. Inside were two nondescript chairs set before a lattice screen. On the other side of the screen was a door. You sat, waited. The door opened, revealing a courtyard. Electa emerged.

Smiling.

She limped to the screen which she threw open with a flourish. I was uncertain what I was supposed to do until Electa said, "Give this old nun a hug!" and she then threw open her arms to make good her invitation.

From there, it became an exchange in which I lamented the countless ways I'd failed that week to live up with what I knew Jesus (and my murky conscience) was asking of me. All of which Electa met with a guffaw, as if I had cracked a joke. I must have looked mystified.

"Blayney," she asked, "have you ever wondered why God went to all the trouble of making you the unusual person you are?"

My blank expression evoked another belly laugh. "It's because God couldn't help Himself," she said, chortling. "God's so in love with you, His creation work couldn't be completed without you."

You can imagine how I looked forward to those weekly meetings.

When I try to picture Jesus, I see Electa. For three years, she never gave up wanting to help me move beyond thinking I would never have an authentic encounter with God until I became a better person.

It was Electa who looked me in the eye one day and

said, "I think I just heard you say you're ready to move on from parish ministry."

I still don't know what I'd said, but it was the start of my tentative, cautious preparing for a new chapter. Electa persuaded me I was ready to taste some of the medicine I'd been prescribing for others the past thirty years, but had tasted precious little for myself.

"Listen to yourself, Blayney," she said, "You're ready to try your wings, fly toward God without requiring the church's imprimatur."

Yes, I longed for a taste of what I had been sponsoring, but for dues-payers, not me. Another instance of the shoemaker's shoeless (discalced?) child.

Now What?

In the years since, I have become at least marginally more comfortable with mystery. More willing to consider Electa's insistence that, even knowing my many shortcomings, I was formed by, and for, God's love.

Five novels, thousands of weekly "Zone Notes" later, the mystery is opaque as ever. Yet, as I near my end, that numinous cloud seems increasingly inviting; gracious, embracing.

I continue to explore those often tumultuous years, no longer feeling the weight of having to wonder if grace really can outsmart human hubris.

Perhaps, if you live this long, you will also marvel at the unforeseen grace that has carried each of us this far.

So many ways, so many unlikely people, God sneaks up on us, nurtures us into deeper places, into mystery we wouldn't dare to venture on our own.

Teachers

Looking back over those years, I see all sorts of invitations to trust intuitive senses of the holy, inhabiting quotidian days. It's fun now to wonder at God subtly opening doors as I walked right by them.

Nineteen seventy-three. Brand new rector. First Arab oil boycott. Cars lined up for blocks, waiting for gas that often ran out before they got to the pump. Inflation heating to 17%. Tensions running high.

On my way home from an evening meeting, I stopped by Faulkner Hospital to visit a parishioner who had terminal cancer. He was in the sleeping porch of the old hospital, an informal setting once used for TB patients. Hard to imagine in today's high tech, high-priced medical world.

Mr. Loring was asleep when I got to his bedside. I wrote a brief note on my calling card, noting the time I was there, saying I hadn't wanted to wake him. In truth I was a little relieved, because it was still uncomfortable for me to find appropriate ways to talk with people who would soon die.

Just as I was about to leave, Loring woke. Big smile, warm greeting in a weak voice.

"Loring," I said, "how are you doing?" I immediately feeling stupid, asking that of a dying man.

His smile widened as he pointed to his distended belly.

"I've got so much gas I feel downright unpatriotic," he said, chuckling.

We both laughed.

"Well, if you could bottle it," I said, "you could make a lot of money."

I prayed with him, made the sign of the cross on his forehead, told him I'd come back again soon.

Next morning his son called me.

"I found your card on Dad's bedside table. Thanks for going to see him? How did he seem to you?"

I described the visit, including the part about his feeling unpatriotic for having so much gas. His son laughed.

"I saw what time you were there," he said. "Dad died less than an hour after you left."

I was stunned. He'd seemed still vital, hardly about to die. His son, a doctor, said he was glad his father seemed cheerful at the end.

"Those must be among the most memorable last words anyone has ever spoken," he said.

I was humbled to have heard his final, cheerful words, and, again, in awe of how we can slip quickly, quietly, from life into death.

Learning Legitimate Authority

I never quite got over wondering if people who turned to me when they were in crisis gave me more authority than was justified. As if I had access to something they didn't, some promise of being able to set things right.

Hard to accept that was a piece of the role, not a measure of my insight or wisdom. Ambassador, bearing gifts from a gracious King.

Agnes and Ernie

Ernie and Agnes, a diminutive couple who lived above the Exxon station in Dedham, somehow found their way to me. Though obviously dirt-poor, they seemed self-sufficient. Hard now to know how old they were. I was in my mid-30s, my first parish as rector. They were probably younger than I am now.

Though they became regulars at worship they didn't mingle with the upper crust Yankees who dominated life in the town and church. In the insulting language of those days, they "knew their place."

Both had health issues. Neither had insurance, nor a sense of how to find medical care. I had recently helped form a hospice at Faulkner Hospital and become friends with Rosemary Ryan, MD, a Medical Mission Sisters nun and our hospice doctor.

Being the caring woman she is, Rosemary agreed to quietly slip Ernie and Agnes through the administrative clutter of medical care and become their doctor, in fact, if off the books.

Agnes came to me one day to tell me Ernie was sick. He was having trouble breathing. I went over to their apartment. Ernie was in bed, clearly in distress, but tried to reassure me.

"I'll be OK. Just a bad cold."

Agnes insisted it was more and it seemed so to me. After much protesting, Ernie agreed to let us take him to be seen by Rosemary.

She checked his vitals, immediately admitted him to the hospital.

Before the afternoon was over, Ernie was moved to intensive care. The next morning he was on a respirator. By afternoon he was unresponsive.

Agnes struggled not to panic. She had come to trust Rosemary, so when Rosemary told her Ernie's kidneys had failed, his heart couldn't keep going without the respirator, she listened.

"But isn't there something you could do to make him better?" she asked.

Rosemary got up from her chair and came around to where Agnes sat, squatted, so she and Agnes were eye level.

"Agnes, no one can say for sure he can't get better, but my best judgment is that he's not going to."

Rosemary remained in that uncomfortable position while Agnes absorbed what to make of this.

"What do we do now?" Agnes asked.

"Let's wait until morning to be sure there's no

change. Then a decision will have to be made about turning off the respirator."

"And he'll die?" Agnes asked.

Long pause. "Yes."

Next morning, I drove Agnes to the hospital. I'd had a phone conversation with Rosemary earlier in which she was clear Ernie couldn't recover.

Rosemary met us at the entrance.

"Is he better?" Agnes asked.

"No, I'm sorry to say, Agnes. His kidneys have completely shut down. Let's go up to the ICU and see him."

Except for losing the little color in his face he'd had the night before, Ernie looked much himself.

Agnes smiled. "He's still breathing."

"The machine is breathing for him, Agnes."

"Is it time to turn off the machine? How long before he dies?"

"I don't know for sure," Rosemary said, "but usually not more than a few minutes. You can tell us when you're ready."

"Can I kiss him? Talk to him? Will he hear me?"

"I think he might hear you."

She walked over to the bed.

"Hi Ernie. I love you." She leaned over, kissed him on the cheek. "Dr. Ryan says it's time to turn off the machine, let you go." She cried quietly. "He looks peaceful."

"I think he is," Rosemary said.

"I think you should turn off the machine."

Rosemary went over and flipped the switch. The three of us stood next to the bed. No words spoken. We watched the heart monitor register Ernie's slowing heart beats.

Just before the line flattened I looked out the window. A young couple walked by, holding hands.

Do you have any idea what's happening up here, just above where you're walking so happily? I thought.

Of course not. Nor should they.

I took out the vial of oil I'd brought, anointed Ernie's forehead. "Unto God's gracious mercy we commit you, Ernie."

I hugged Agnes. Rosemary hugged her. Agnes cried a little more, still quietly.

"Thank you," she said to us, "you made Ernie's trip to heaven start beautifully."

I checked in on Agnes a couple of times a week. One day, a month or so after Ernie died, I went by the apartment. Agnes wasn't there. I asked the gas station attendant if he'd seen her.

"Saw her briefly yesterday. Today, when she hadn't come down at her usual time, I went up to check. All her things were gone."

I never knew where she went. Nor, for that matter, where Ernie went. I knew they were sent to teach me how to meet our biggest mystery since our birth.

That she disappeared as mysteriously as she and Ernie had first appeared, made them seem like angels we read about in ancient scripture. Angels are God's messengers. Agnes trusted God with Ernie, even while sorrowing at his dying. So much still to learn from these angels.

I don't measure my vocation only by being faced with death, but tending peoples' dying deeply accented my sense of the significance, purpose, of ordained life. Becoming willing, however reluctantly, to look into the face of eternity. Maybe only doctors and undertakers see it as often.

Their vocations are a little different from mine. Doctors, understandably, often see death as their failure to cure. Not rational, they may understand, but the emotional impact of having failed to heal, can be strong.

Faith in What Remains

In Dedham I became friends with the family who ran the local funeral parlor. Their unfailing compassion impressed me. Not only their professional manner, but that they never became calloused about their hard job. Never considered helping people through that hard time routine.

One brother told me he understood that he was hired to take care of what most in our death-denying culture, avoid. That set me to thinking about what I did. Being aware of my own foibles, the authority people gave me could seem undeserved. It took years for me to understand they conferred that authority on me, not because they judged me trustworthy (though I think/ hope many did), but because they were asking me, and I agreed, to muck around in the sticky places that we normally do all we can to avoid.

The Folsom family were unfailingly professional, compassionate, helping people walk through their grief. Like Sister Electa, they became my teachers.

All In This Together

Several years later, standing at the door of the La Jolla church, greeting parishioners as they left Sunday worship, a loud crash interrupted the greetings. A car had crashed. A woman had been thrown from her car and was lying on the grass.

I rushed over, wasn't sure if she was alive. Putting my hand on her forehead, I said the prayer I had come to use when mortality seems fragile.

"Undo God's gracious mercy and protection, we commit you ..."

She opened one eye. "How did you know I was Jewish?" she asked. I laughed. "I didn't," I said. "We Christians use Aaron's prayer too."

Happy to say, she turned out not to be badly injured. And I learned, again, that we humans have more in common even with those whose traditions can make them seem different, incomprehensible, than we usually recognize.

Pathology That Won't Heal

Two in the morning, the phone rings.

"Can you come bail me out?"

Daniel (not his real name) was an active member of the parish. He had been on the search committee that brought me there. He sang in the choir, sat on the vestry, organized and oversaw the acolytes, mostly young boys (a few girls) who assisted at worship.

He was funny, sardonic, clever. Fun.

Daniel had been arrested on a warrant accusing him of molesting boys.

He was in the county jail across from the church. I went over. He was not eligible for bail until a judge could hear the case in the morning. I assured him I would stick with him through whatever lay ahead.

Released on bond, required to enter counseling, not have anything to do with boys, he reported weekly to a probation officer.

The mother who swore out the complaint agreed

not to press the matter further so long as she could be assured he was under scrutiny.

Though his shame caused him to drop away from the church, Daniel continued to come see me to talk about how it was going. He described the averse conditioning in which he wired his genitals and anytime he experienced a sexual feeling for a boy, gave himself what he described to me as a powerful jolt.

"How often do you have to do that?" I asked him.

"Hundreds of times a day."

"Wow, do you think it is quieting your compulsion?"

"No."

This went on for a couple of years. Daniel even checked himself into a facility that treated his disorder.

Daniel never considered it a disorder.

I consulted a psychiatrist who specialized in treating pedophiles. "There's no cure," she said. "Some manage to keep from acting out, the way an alcoholic can discipline himself to keep from drinking. But those addictions aren't curable. In fact, if honest, many of them will tell you they believe it's our uptight culture that's the problem, not their love for boys.

"I love those boys," Daniel told me "Our culture has a hang-up about sex. The ancient Greeks and Romans honored love between men and boys."

"Maybe so, Daniel, but this isn't ancient Greece. Whether you think it's honorable or not, carrying on will end with you in prison for a long time."

The old wisdom about God condemning the sin while loving the sinner cut no ice with Daniel. He was uncommonly bright, articulate, and never gave up trying to persuade me that my cultural bias was keeping me from seeing how good his loving those boys was for them.

One day he came to see me, seeming happier than usual.

"Good news you'll be glad to hear," he began. "I've fallen in love with a wonderful woman, and intend to marry her."

As the story unfolded I realized I knew the woman, a divorcee with two boys the age Daniel was attracted to. He asked for my blessing.

"I can't give you my blessing for this, Daniel. In fact, I will do what I must to make sure that marriage never happens."

Without a goodbye he walked out.

The next day at a convention at the Cathedral in downtown Boston, I was summoned for an urgent phone call.

It was Steve, one of the few who had continued to stay in touch with Daniel.

"Daniel shot himself last night."

I wonder how that could have been different? Did Daniel make the only choice open to him?

I still don't quite dare think suicide is a better choice than enduring something anti-social, harmful, addictive. Could you consider that in the same light as suffering a horrific painful illness?

How does that square with claiming God's love is more powerful than the worst sin we can imagine?

What does it mean to claim God's love will set right all the pathology that can seem so pervasive? What about alcoholism? Pedophilia?

What do we mean when we say that after Jesus' resurrection, the sting of death has lost its power over us?

I can believe no one is beyond reach of God's love, but there seem some pathologies that even strong, determined people can't overcome. Pathology so dense even God's love can't penetrate?

I confess I thought I might understand Daniel's suicide, knowing that his pedophilia, seemingly beyond his ability (or willingness) to inhibit, meant his future was bound to be bleak. Destructive.

When I preached at Daniel's funeral I couldn't bring myself to say that he may have made the bravest, maybe the only choice finally open to him.

It requires counting on God's love reaching beyond the grave. Somehow setting right things that couldn't be set right in life. Is that fantasy I entertain to soften hopelessness? Helplessness? I choose to consider it a legitimate choice for some. It scares the daylights out of me to admit that.

Can Everyone Be Saved?

I was often taken to task for insisting that nothing can separate us from God's love. (cf. Romans 8). I tried to be clear that didn't mean everything would always turn out all right by our measure, but that as whoever wrote the Letter to the Romans, put it: "I am persuaded that neither death nor life, nor angels nor principalities nor powers, nor things present nor things to come, nor height nor depth, nor any other created thing, shall be able to separate us from the love of God."

In other words, God gets the last word. And the last word is, "I love you, no matter what. And will never let you go."

"You're preaching license," I was warned. "If people listen to you they'll think anything goes, no limits." I allowed as how, on every basis by which we measure things, that was undeniable.

What About Hitler?

I fretted about that. In my discomfort I was granted a vision. Or something akin to one. A dream?

Took me a moment to realize I was standing behind God's throne. And that this was judgment day.

A man stood before God for judgment.

His Charlie Chaplin mustache made him unmistakable: Adolph Hitler.

Hitler shook his fist at God. "Go ahead, send me to hell," he shouted. "I'm not afraid of you. Or the devil."

God's voice was modulated, low. I had to strain to hear it: "Not so fast, Adolph. There's work to be done before this is settled."

Suddenly a little girl, maybe seven, materialized. I somehow recognized her. She'd died in the gas chamber at Auschwitz. She walked over to Hitler, said, "Hello Adolph. It didn't work."

She embraced him. He stiffened, squirmed, tried to turn away.

"No!" Hitler shouted, "I'm not doing this. Just send me to hell. Now."

As the girl walked away an old woman approached him, said, and did, the same as the little girl had."

Hitler began sobbing. "I don't have to put up with this shit. I know where I belong. Just get it done."

"Well, Adolph," God said gently, "we've got seven million more to go. Then we'll see how it works out."

I once told this story in a sermon. A few loved it, several were appalled. Many were mystified.

Mystified best describes what an encounter with God's unconditional love has to be like. It can be bloody uncomfortable and disrupt how we understand things.

When you come clean with someone, acknowledge hard-edged reality about something good manners say to keep quiet, it feels dicey.

Only the Blind
Can Sometimes Lead the Blind

Ann stumbled down the three steps to my office, visibly drunk. It was 10 o'clock in the morning. She said she wanted to talk about what an unfeeling bastard her husband was.

Before she got much further, I interrupted her.

"Ann, you're drunk. Why don't you go home, sober up. We can talk later."

"Aren't you a fine priest!" she slurred. Got up, nearly tipped over, and stormed out.

She rebuffed my phone calls. A month or so later she came back to see me. Sober.

"I want to thank you for being blunt with me," she said. "Everyone has been dancing around my drinking, not wanting to rock the boat.

"I left here chagrined that I was so obviously drunk. I'd thought I was pretty good at hiding it."

She went on to tell me she had begun AA, found a sponsor, and had been sober for two weeks. I congratulated her. Told her I hated confronting her.

"It's your job," she said.

Six months later Ann came again, still sober.

"When someone comes to talk with you about their drinking," she said, "tell them you're not equipped to help them with that. I got lucky, ran into a friend I hadn't known who was a drunk. She led me to AA. Tell them you have the names and numbers of several alcoholics who can help. Drinking alcoholics are among the world's most clever, manipulative people. They'll run circles around you while you think you're being a caring pastor."

I took her at her word. God's love never ends. Our hard-headed attempts to prove ourselves unworthy, may not be as dramatic as Hitler's, but we all have our ways. Until some intervention breaks through our resistance.

Who wouldn't welcome the news that God loves us, no matter what?

Every one of us, that's who. It flies in the face of common sense. Trusting the power of love, of redemption, requires facing down the powerful SSI—shitty self-image—so many of us have habituated. Who knows why so many of us carry that burden?

Maybe Philip Larkin nailed it in his poem, "This Be the Verse":

They fuck you up, your mum and dad.
    They may not mean to, but they do. . . .

As good an explanation as any, as if an explanation has an impact on our resistance to more good news than we can dare to trust. Or think we deserve.

Wounded Healer

A clergy support group were my most valued colleagues. I can't remember the issue I was talking about. I was bouncing off the bottom of despair and self-loathing. I must have gone on at some length.

Finally, one of them interrupted me.

"Let me be sure I've got this straight, Blayney. You believe God loves everyone who has ever lived, or ever will. Nothing anyone can do is terrible enough to sever that love.

"With the possible exception of Blayney? Do I have that right? You must consider yourself awfully special."

He had it right.

How do I know that God's love overpowers everything, even the Holocaust? Even my narcissism, thinking my sins so different, so special, they're unforgivable?

I don't. That's a decision. I began testing it at some point, based on my admiration for a few clergy who made that claim the heart of their ministry. I experienced God's transforming love, not surprisingly, from people who trusted me, telling me something they'd used everything in their power to keep anyone from discovering.

Not me, I finally understood, but the role my vocation, God's initiative, had assigned me. Bearer and announcer of love that finally overpowers the worst in us.

I hope you, too, have had someone love you so powerfully, when you felt particularly unloved, that it changed the way you felt about yourself.

It can take all the wiles you can muster.

Outsmarting Love – Defying

A colleague was visited by a mob-member from another city. The man had been diagnosed with terminal cancer. He wanted to get some things off his chest. His training would have taken him to a Roman Catholic priest for confession, but he thought the Church was too entwined with the Mob for him to trust. He came to the next best thing, an Episcopal priest, hoping he might find absolution there.

He had killed other mobsters. The steely manner he had developed to do what his life demanded unless he wanted to end up dead himself, gave way when he described a murder in which he had accidentally killed a nearby child.

The priest listened compassionately, spoke about repentance, requiring changing, softening his steely façade, working at setting things right. "Hard thing is you can't set things right with people you've killed," my colleague told him.

"God still loves you, but you have to allow God to break down your resistance, so you and God can work out your forgiveness."

The man looked puzzled. "You mean God doesn't hate me for what I did?"

"No. God hates what you did, but not you. Only God has the power to set it right. I have been given the power to assure you God hasn't given up on you, will never give up on you. But I don't have the power to help you set it right with those you killed."

The man pulled a pistol from under his jacket, set it on the desk between them. "If I ever thought you'd told anyone about this conversation, I wouldn't hesitate to kill you."

My quick-witted colleague, said, "I'll put a note in my safe deposit box about this meeting. I will explain that if something happens to me, they should go looking for you."

The man looked startled. Then he smiled. "Guess we're in sort of the same line of work," he said. "Keeping confidences about life and death. You'd have made a fine mobster."

Dying Practice

I used to wonder if it were possible, or a good idea, to practice dying. Sounds bizarre, self-defeating, when all our conditioning is about surviving.

What if as close an encounter with my death as I can experience before it visits me, rather than being demoralizing, turns out to enhance the precious, unearned gift of being here?

Doug came looking for me after church one day. He introduced himself.

"I'm Doug. I just moved here. I'm a forensic pathologist. I'm gay, with a partner. I've got AIDS. I'll be dead within a year. Where do I go for a support group?"

I must have looked blank.

"Oh, so I have to start it," he said.

He did. It came to be called the Blessed Group. (Blessed are those who mourn, for they shall be comforted. Matthew 5:4)

To my surprise, when we let it be known that a group would be meeting for those with a terminal diagnosis, or close to someone dying, six or eight people turned up.

Doug became our inspiration. As his illness progressed he described what he was experiencing the way a pathologist might describe a body he was dissecting. Once we got used to Doug's unnerving calm, matter-of-factness, about his own deterioration, his candor, calm courage, humor, it became infectious.

He inspired us to watch the progress of aging and illness in ourselves, honestly, finding meaning, even humor, in what we would once have thought morbid.

The receptionist who sat at a desk just outside the room where we met told me people asked what was going on in that room where all the raucous laughter was coming from.

"Oh, they're all dying," became her favorite response.

"I'm practicing dying," Doug told us one day.

"Say more," we begged.

"When I'm going to sleep I imagine giving my feet away. Then my legs. I'm almost up to my privates," he said with a belly laugh, which we joined in.

The Blessed Group met at Doug's house the two meetings before he died. Mostly comatose, confined to his bed, his dogs were on the bed snuggled against him. I told him we were there. He smiled, managed a weak greeting.

I asked him if his practicing dying seemed helpful now. He smiled again.

"Yes," he said, his voice so quiet it was hard to hear, "but different than I imagined."

We were eager to hear more. But Doug had used what little energy remained to him. A couple of days later his partner called to say Doug was near the end. I went, prayed over him. He even smiled one more time. He died before I left.

Doug left his mark on the Blessed Group. And powerfully on me. Our take on our own dying entered a new dimension. Being together with people who engaged, rather than fending off, that reality, turned out to be, not depressing, but life-giving.

A man a couple of years younger than I am now, who had multiple cancer recurrences, told us: "I only buy those little travel size tubes of toothpaste."

We are wonderfully designed. If things go well, we may flourish for close to a hundred years. The unfathomable collection of cells that organize themselves into us have a shelf-life. As we near that best-buy time, we can be grateful for what we were given. Those cells keep finding new, unexpected ways to rich up our ongoing life.

Our ego pushes back against the notion that the identity we've inhabited is for a season. Learning to stare down ego's efforts to persuade us we're irreplaceable requires unaccustomed discipline.

Tough, but possible to let go, the illusion ego is so clever at seducing us into, denying our fragility, mortality. Learning to let it go the way of all illusion. Smoke and mirrors, our finally, mysteriously evaporating into the ether.

Trusting God, embracing love-energy, the gift given to all of us, learn to spend it, maybe even recklessly, give it away.

Radical freedom is breaking the bonds of ego's demands.

Acknowledging our end helps with that holy work. No need to squander energy hoping to postpone moving from these uncharted waters to the upcoming uncharted waters.

Aren't Priests Supposed to Be Prescient?

Weird, hard, getting used to inhabiting the role of shaman, holy man, people assuming you have mystical powers.

Like knowing things, innately, by some sacred osmosis.

Madeleine L'Engle, the author of *A Wrinkle in Time*, was injured in a car accident in San Diego. She was in hospital. Someone who visited her called me, and told me that said she wanted to see me.

"Where have you been?" was her greeting when I went into her hospital room. I knew better than to try to explain I hadn't known she was in town, let alone in an accident. Had I ever met her? Maybe. I knew her then son-in-law, Alan Jones, Dean of Grace Cathedral in San Francisco.

"I'm so sorry," I said, "I would have come sooner, had I known."

"It's been in the paper that I was in an accident."

"Sorry, I missed it."

She'd been banged around, but seemed to be mostly intact. She wanted unction for healing, and by some unlikely luck I had brought a chrism of oil to anoint her. That seemed to soften her pique at my not having come sooner. We fell into conversation about many things. Among them, Alan Jones.

Alan and I were the final two candidates for Dean of San Francisco. He was a better choice than I would have been. Born and educated in England, he'd been a faculty member at General Seminary in NYC. He was smarter, better educated, and most important, more sophisticated, which counted in San Francisco, which considers itself a pocket of urbane sanity in the midst of California edginess.

"I once asked Alan," I told Madeleine, "if he believed in hell. I've gotten myself into hot water with parishioners for not seeming to believe people go to hell for having done bad things."

She smiled. "Can't wait to hear what Alan said."

"He said he thought it was required of orthodox Christians to believe in hell. 'But I don't think we have to believe anyone spends eternity there.'"

"Dear Alan," Madeleine said, "ever the 20th century casuist."

Casuistry, often associated with Hebrew *midrash*, means the taking ancient religious texts and giving them new meaning that fits better with contemporary thought.

Clever escape for me, insisting that God's love rules and overrules the worst in us.

I might have said that Hitler spent a long time in hell while he was confronted with seven million people who died in the Holocaust. Is it pollyannish to think Hitler might have repented; been reunited with his victims? His better angels? Depends on whether you think God actually has the power and will to overcome the worst in us.

Or on whether you give a damn about such an arcane issue. Or are willing to let your mind wander into arenas we rarely visit.

I do. Passionately.

Maintaining even a semblance of trust in the promises of religion, any religion, requires unending revision of what our senses report back to us as we navigate the world. We children of the post-post-enlightenment, powerfully conditioned to doubt, dismiss what lies beyond our agreed-on boundaries of reality.

Most of us, aware of the mysteries physics and space travel, have uncovered, accept that reality is more complex than our senses record. But the invisible, unknowable, ineffable God, requires another layer of intellectual surrender.

For people like me, calling Jesus God's incarnation (*in carne*, flesh), helps. For sophisticated Greeks and Romans, in the centuries following Jesus' death, the idea of God in human flesh was considered an intellectual scandal, a denial of agreed-on reality.

All these centuries later, I'm aware that's still true for maybe most of those in the pews on Sunday. Trying to preach without dumbing down, while understanding that most people's sense of God and Jesus, stalled in Sunday School, is a challenge.

In recent years a number of what previously were considered arcane practices, limited to mystics and monks, have become more usual.

Meditation For Dummies

During my tenure at the Dedham, Massachusetts parish, I met with a small (4-6) group once a week at 6:00 A.M., for meditation. We sat on the floor of my office, some chanting (*ohm*), mostly silence, for an hour.

There was an unusual makeup of people: a senior partner in a major investment firm, a special education teacher, a banker., and a few others came from time to time. Each of them sought me out to talk about what we were doing in those early mornings.

"Would you call it prayer?" One wondered.

"Sometimes I feel like I'm sort of floating into another dimension for a while; do you think that's real?"

"It's about the only time in my week when I stop fretting about all the shit that keeps coming at me."

One morning, Stokely, the investment banker, and I arrived a few minutes early. As I unlocked the door to the parish hall and we walked in, there was the noise of someone scurrying around.

A young woman, buck-naked, ran by us, down the stairs and into the bathroom. Stokely and I stood silently for a moment trying to figure out if we had really seen what we had seen.

Stokely broke the silence.

"Don't tell anyone about this," he said, "or next week there will be a mob coming for meditation."

The high-school aged, young man I hired as sexton while our usual sexton was in hospital, had found a happy place to romance his girlfriend.

And Stokely and I reconsidered the meaning of God visiting us in human flesh.

"She went by too fast to get a really good look," Stokely said, "but enough to see she was quite beautiful. God is good!"

Maybe you won't be surprised that Stokely's son, Amor, who inherited his father's sense of life's surprises, has become one of our nation's best-selling novelists.

Jesus and the Thief

Even infused by it, as we are, Incarnation—God hanging out with us—always surprises.

I rose at 4:30 A.M., Easter morning, to walk down to church for the major festival when we would see by far the most people of the year. Many we would not see again until next Easter. I found it especially exciting to try to connect with those unfamiliar with the liturgy and story behind it.

I stopped by the coffee shop for a tea to get me started. The waitress was agitated.

"Someone stole my purse," she said. "I know it had to be that homeless guy who was just here."

I commiserated with her, then went on to church. As I went into the nave I smelled smoke. Following the scent to the side porch I discovered a man sleeping. He had started a fire from scraps of paper and refuse he'd taken from the trash. Next to him was a woman's purse.

He didn't wake right away when I called to him. I nudged him several times before he stirred. He looked confused, hung over. I began stomping out the fire.

As he gradually came around, he began apologizing.

"I just wanted to get warm. Never thought it would get so big."

"And how about that purse?" I asked.

"Purse? I have no idea."

"I suspect you do. I was just in the coffee shop and the waitress told me her purse had been stolen. Want to go back with me, return it to her, or should I call the cops?"

"No, don't call the cops. I'll go back with you."

We did. The waitress looked angry when she saw us come in, then spotted the purse which he was carrying.

"You son-of-a-bitch. You walked off with my purse. What the hell did you think you were doing?"

"Sorry," he said, "I really didn't mean to. I was drunk, didn't know what I was doing."

"Yeah, well, maybe you can get the cops to believe that. I don't."

"I don't know if you'll go along with this," I said, "Can't blame you if you don't. I told him if he came back with me and apologized, returned your purse, I wouldn't call the cops."

"I don't know," she said, "my money, license, credit cards, everything, is in that purse. It would have wrecked my life for a month."

She checked her purse, relieved: "Looks like it's all here."

The thief looked down at his feet, silent.

"It's Easter," I said. "Jesus was crucified between two thieves who first mocked him, then begged him for forgiveness. I'm not Jesus, and neither are you, I understand, but might you be willing to not call the cops. If only because it's Easter?"

The thief started quietly weeping.

"I was hungry, cold, afraid, drunk," he said. "That's no excuse. I hate myself for this."

She seemed to soften.

"Only because the Reverend asked me to."

"How about I fund his breakfast?" I asked, reaching into my pocket, pulled out a $10 bill.

His weeping turned to sobs.

"OK," she said.

"I've got to get to church," I said. "Have a good breakfast. Next time you need something this bad, come see me."

The sexton was cleaning the porch when I got there. I explained what had happened.

He laughed. "Guess you don't need to light the traditional first fire of Easter. Your Jesus, thief friend took care of it."

I junked the sermon I'd spent the week preparing for the most significant festival of the year. I preached instead about Jesus showing up in the least imaginable form: a homeless man, a thief, inadvertently lighting the *Paschal* (Passover) fire.

I said Jesus forgave the thief who was crucified alongside him even after the priest mocked Jesus for being powerless to save himself.

Several told me how moved they were by the story. How it brought a new dimension to their understanding of Jesus. One woman was neither moved nor amused.

"You had the biggest congregation of the year, eager to hear you preach resurrection. But no, you didn't even prepare a sermon. You told that stupid, scandalous story instead."

When God shows up in human flesh the script has to be rewritten.

Belief, the Booby Prize

Sometimes people screw up their courage and come right out and ask me, "Do you really believe in God?" Before I decide how to address that, there usually comes the next question: "Do you believe in life after death?" The two questions seem connected in our minds.

First question: It's a decision I made somewhere along the way. I can cite a lot of what went into the decision, but in the end, it's about what I make of being here. No, I don't believe in a "being" called God. It's about whether I trust that Love (God's real name) has the final word. More powerful than all the obstacles we put on Love's way.

I understand that answer doesn't satisfy a lot of people. Until one makes the decision for herself, I don't think it's possible to address it. The question poses itself over and over.

Life after death? Maybe, who knows? Have to wait and see.

God? Scratch the surface of pretty much any one of us and you'll find doubt about self-worth. If you're willing to consider God/Love as more powerful than all the stuff we put in the way of love, then I say you're a believer.

I might ask if you have liked being here, if you are, on balance, glad that egg and sperm got together, or whether you would just as soon have skipped it. If you said you're glad to have been here, I would say that makes you a believer. Like the multitudes who have tried to make language about the ineffable, affirming the value of being given life strikes me as the true test.

The Spy and the Priest

A childhood friend who became an even closer friend in our old age, helped me put flesh on that mystery.

Howard and I were classmates in 7th and 8th grades in the American School in Manila. We left together for a boy's boarding school in Connecticut. For different reasons we each left after 10th grade. Howard, because his father had business reverses and couldn't afford the tuition.

I flunked out.

For its 50th reunion our class went looking for lost members. They found Howard and me, and we found each other.

To my astonishment Howard turned out to be among the most highly decorated undercover agents in the history of the CIA. (Unknown to most, because in the CIA even your honors remain secret. Howard pointed out, amusedly, that in the clandestine service you have to leave your decorations behind.)

He was equally astonished to discover I had been a parish priest. ("Are you fucking kidding me?" was his first question.)

Fascinated, not only by our disparate lives, but by the surprisingly fierce bond we re-established over the ensuing few years before Howard died.

My 5th novel, *The Spy and the Priest*, was my attempt to unpack that fascination.

Our exchanges opened a new dimension in my sense of vocation: of trusting God; what that vocation is, how it works.

Howard was more conventionally pious than I, though no longer a church-goer.

I visited him in his retirement hideaway high atop a mountain, accessible only by a treacherous, narrow, winding road. As I learned more about his life and career, I could see why he chose such a remote, difficult-to-reach place.

He greeted me with a bear hug.

I was moved but uneasy at his so quickly putting more trust in me than I was sure was justified.

Every corner of the living space in his house was filled with assault weapons.

"I've got one from every war this country ever fought, including the Revolutionary War," he said. He picked up a musket gun, to confirm his claim.

"Howard," I said, "what the hell prompted you to collect all this stuff?"

"Never understood the stock market," he said, "considered it a roulette game. But weapons? The market for weapons never falters."

Before Howard died he began donating his collection to a museum. Turned out he had the most complete collection of assault weapons in private hands. The museum added a wing and named it for Howard and his wife.

"You're my oldest friend," he said, "I've decided to trust you in ways I haven't trusted anyone for many years."

He described one close call in which he ended up killing two men before they were able to kill him. He went to a drawer and pulled out the pistol he'd used in that deadly encounter

"Here," he said, extending it out to me.

I must have flinched. "I'm not much on weapons," I said. "We never had them in my house growing up."

"I suppose you're a pacifist," Howard said, his voice tinged with sarcasm.

"No," I said, "I don't have the discipline pacifism requires."

"If you want us to be real friends," Howard said, "you need to handle this weapon. You need to fire it so you can have a sense of what it feels like. Imagine what a sacred piece it is for me. Saved my life. It means as much to me as your communion chalice must to you."

We went out onto his balcony from which there was a long view across the Shenandoah valley.

"I've loaded in a few little 22 caliber shells. Won't give you much kick. Just aim for those rocks."

My hand shook. I tried to pull the trigger slowly as Howard instructed. The gun flew up as I fired, nearly hitting me in the nose.

Howard laughed.

"So much for your combat training. Best stay clear of any firefight. Hold it in both hands, arms extended. See if you can hit that rock."

At his insistence I fired twice more, finally able to hold the pistol somewhat steady.

"Might need a little more practice," he said, clearly enjoying himself, "but I can see you've got the right stuff."

We genuinely and powerfully liked and respected each other. Gradually I got it that, for Howard, there was an extra dimension to our friendship.

Being a spy not only forced him with having to kill, but lie, even betray people. He had been willing to do that because of his profound sense of patriotism, and his duty seemed to him to require it.

He told me he came to put his trust in force, the only thing he thought people respected.

He had a religious confidence that it was God's protection that saw him through his perilous life. But his traditional piety caused him anxiety about whether how he'd spent his life had put his soul in eternal jeopardy.

He was afraid of being sent to hell. Forever.

How we torture ourselves carrying this image of an angry, punishing father, an image largely a projection of our own mistrust of our own worth, and of the power of forgiving love.

After many fits and starts, Howard came right out and told me his fear of eternal damnation. I was incredulous. Sophisticated, worldly, cynical, he clung to what I consider a vestigial, medieval view of life.

And death. Medieval maybe, but palpable for Howard.

It took me a while to trust our friendship enough to speak candidly about all that.

"Howie, I just don't think the old ways we understood judgment—heaven, hell—portrays the matter in ways that can help us make sense of the way I understand it to be with God. That was about a vengeful, tribal, God. Not the merciful God whose love for all of us is unbreakable. Even by the worst we can do. God doesn't give up on us.

"That's what the Jesus story means: God's love for us has no bounds. The worst we can do will be set right in the end."

Initially, that angered Howard.

"I get it," he said, biting off his words, "you spent 30 years as a priest but you don't actually believe in God. Not the God we all learned about. Wow. I thought being a spy required me to lie a lot. Congratulations to you for being an even better liar than me. You would have made a great spy."

That stung.

Howard was a hard-headed realist. What you see is what you get. Nuances are attempts to fudge reality in your favor.

As I age, less and less seems simply what it appears. Nuance pervades every iota of reality for me.

The last time we saw each other I wrapped my white stole around my shoulders, then around Howard's and my hands, and gave Howard absolution. I explained that he and God, and those two people he killed, would find ways to set things right. As the Bible says, with God all things are possible. Including restoring what we seem to have destroyed.

"But," I assured him (and myself), "God doesn't make mistakes in creating anyone. God finds ways to set right what we can't. Our job is to keep trust in God's willingness and ability to do that. And to try to learn that radical forgiveness for each other."

It's a reach for all of us. No one convicts us more mercilessly than we convict ourselves. Episcopalians can be cynical about fundamentalism, thinking ourselves smarter, more sophisticated. But I don't think we're very different from fundamentalists in knowing we haven't lived up to what we think God wants of us. Or what we want for ourselves. We're all longing to be set free of our shame and disappointment at how far short we fall.

I was never sure whether Howard thought I had the authority to pronounce his absolution. Or whether God's love really would set right all the horror Howard had seen and been a part of. More than ever before those times with Howard upped the ante for the importance of my conviction that Love is finally more powerful than hate.

I made two trips to Howard's hideaway on that mountaintop in the Shenandoah of rural Virginia. We laughed about our adolescent adventures, marveling at how our lives had evolved so differently.

Or had they?

Howard spent the first five years of his life in a

Japanese concentration camp in the Philippines. When
he tried to explain what had drawn him to work for
the CIA, he described having nearly starved before
being rescued by American paratroopers who stormed
the camp as the Japanese were about to execute all the
American prisoners.

He remembered a young Lieutenant picking him up
"like a sack of potatoes, slinging me onto his hip, as he
ran, dodging flying bullets. He said to me, 'Son, you're
going to be all right. I'm taking you home.'"

"I figured," Howard said, "if my life was worth anything, I should give it to the country that saved it."

Did My Early Trauma Have That Power?

Though perhaps lacking the drama of Howard's discovery of his vocation, I told him where I thought mine had its beginning.

I told him about my dog, Birdie's, death, when I was 8 years old—the same year my father commissioned me as his surrogate in being the "man in the family."

"Reverend, Rightor," Gertrude said, "you got to come. Now!"

He did.

He gave that afternoon to me and my grief. Grief, a key, mostly unwelcome, ingredient in the recipe for tasting life's sweetness. For discovering resources in ourselves we never knew.

A year after Birdie's death, I landed in hospital with an inflamed appendix requiring surgery. My parents were away visiting my grandparents. They made a quick trip home. Arriving in my hospital room in the middle of the night they found Mr. Rightor in a chair next to my bed, sound asleep.

He was, and is, who the lieutenant was for Howard.

I was uncomfortable comparing my dog's death with Howard's near death in a Japanese prison camp. But Howard listened intently to my story.

"You know," he said, "the measure of those moments probably isn't how heroic they may have been, but how they played out in the rest of our lives.

"The way you describe it I'd say Mr. Rightor and that Lieutenant were God's messengers, telling us our lives mattered, and we ought to use them well."

"Hole shit," Howard, "I wish I'd been that clear, that eloquent, in trying to make sense of my vocation. Do you know that angels are considered God's messengers? You and I were visited by angels who showed us the way we were to go."

Howard remains a critical character in the list of those who have taught me more about my vocation than I had any idea when I showed up for ordination.

Life Tends to Level Intensity

Life became infinitely more subtle, complex, ambiguous, over the next 60 years. Much in those years clouded the clarity of those early traumas. As Howard and I exchanged stories about our early lives, our conviction deepened that those early traumas had fused our peculiar vocations in our bones. It was as if the ensuing decades were the unfolding of what we intuitively sensed in those childhood experiences.

Episcopal Welfare

Something I only vaguely understood about how God's grace can be lived out seems oddly illuminated in the early days of Joe Biden's presidency.

And maybe explains why Biden's agenda, and the promise of God's love transcending all the things that we deplore, in others, and maybe more, in ourselves, and why it is so hard to believe.

At my ordination as parish priest, an ancient guild, I was slotted into a system from which the western world has largely moved on over the past generation.

You could call it an ecclesiastical welfare system.

Along with housing provided by the church, I received a car allowance, a discretionary fund for helping people in trouble, health care, a pension funded by the parish (which must set aside 8% of my annual stipend) matched by the pension fund which had a handsome corpus. It was begun back in the early 20th century by Bishop Lawrence of Massachusetts who said clergy had to continue working until they died or spend old age in penury. He asked J.P. Morgan to help begin a fund that, at last count, totaled many billions of dollars.

A retired colleague told me that when he says his prayers at night he thanks God for giving him another day of life, and J.P. Morgan for making him able to afford it.

I have been supported by a liberal welfare system, which the country has been systematically divesting itself of since Reagan became president in 1981. He set out to persuade us that government is the enemy of a well-run society.

That agenda has become the mainstay of the Republican Party. At the close of WWII, the Republican Party dedicated itself to conserving a sense of thrift and providing for clever entrepreneurs to accumulate wealth, within the context of an economy that provided a safety net for people who, for whatever reason, slip into poverty.

The moment in which I am writing this (spring, 2021), President Biden is proposing a bold initiative to renew the promise of government to insure the well-being of all its citizens. Maybe by the time you're reading this it will be clearer whether he even partially succeeded. Or like most attempts in recent years to build security into the lives of everyone, was a political reach too far. And he may have been returned to private life.

Am I bold enough to claim a particular political agenda is in keeping with Christian/Jewish thinking about how things should be structured?

Well, yes. With many caveats, lest I simply pit my God-vision against that of evangelicals who enlist God in discriminating against dark-skinned people and immigrants. I am cautious in claiming to know God's will. Yet caring for people in need seems more in keeping with what I understand of God, than does winnowing them out of God's care.

As many have pointed out, where we took a wrong turn in western Christianity was when we began to worship Jesus rather than follow Jesus.

"I was hungry, and you fed me. Naked and you clothed me. Sick and you visited me. Homeless and you sheltered me. Downcast and you lifted me up." (My translation).

We say, "I don't remember that?"

"Inasmuch as you did it to one of the least of these, you did it to me," Jesus explains.

While I wouldn't go so far as to claim Jesus as a member of the Democratic Party, it seems clear to me that he wouldn't subscribe to the naked capitalist notion of everyone for herself.

What is it like when a moment summons your best self? Better self than you ever imagined you have resources for? Calling on divine energy, invested in everyone, so easily buried beneath ego and ambition? Divine because, while we may be able to imagine it, putting it into practice so often seems beyond our ingenuity, or even sheer grit.

How might it look to consider it the obligation of government, any government regardless of ideology, to see to the basic needs of everyone?

Dying On the City

Working in a Washington, D.C. church, across Lafayette Square from the White House, where the naked battle for power was focused, I received a call one day from a friend who edited a small, counter-cultural weekly newspaper on Capitol Hill.

"There is a woman holed up in a residential hotel downtown," he said. "She won't open the door for cops or social workers or anyone else. They assume she's mentally ill, maybe starving. All she's told them is that she's a parishioner of your church. Do you think you might be able to persuade her to let someone in to help her?"

I spent most of the next several days trying to help Eva Mae Mahon. She did let me into her apartment (sometimes authority can be used for good), even agreed to go to the hospital. She never left the hospital. She was old and frail but she hadn't been expected to die just then.

Seems the hospital was preparing discharge papers for her. When I asked later where they were discharging her to, no one could answer.

The nurse had brought her clothes for her to dress, then leave. The nurse told her she would come back to take her down to the hospital entrance.

When the nurse returned 15 minutes later Eva Mae was lying face-down on the bed. Dead.

I admire the will of someone who can choose to die when all she can see ahead is misery.

She was on welfare. There was public money to bury her. I arranged with the undertaker for a cloth coffin. Because she was being buried within 2 days there was no need to embalm her body.

I showed up at the paupers' cemetery vested in cassock, surplice, white stole—white for resurrection. Was led by the caretaker to a corner of the lot where two burly men had dug a grave. They were leaning on their shovels waiting for me to get through my duties so they could finish theirs.

I greeted them, thanked them for being there. "This lady's name is Eva Mae Mahon," I said. "She was poor and sorrowful. She had no family, no friends. I wonder if you might be kind enough to be her friends today, so even though there will be no marker on her grave she will at least have been acknowledged, honored by you, and by me?"

I'm sure they did this often. Eva Mae was the first person I had ever buried without a single mourner present. Without hesitating the two men stepped alongside

me next to the grave, removed their hats, and still leaning on their shovels, solemnly bowed their heads.

Aware they were hourly employees, this probably
was not their only burial that day (there had been three
other corpses of indigent people at the undertaker), I
sang the *Nunc Dimittis*—"Lord, now lettest Thou Thy
servant depart in peace"—said prayers for the dead,
commended her soul to God, and stepped back, nod-
ding to the two men that they could now lower the
coffin and fill in the grave.

After the coffin was lowered, one asked me, "Would
you like to throw a handful of dirt in her grave?"

I did. I was filled with emotion. I stood silently
while one of them drove the front-end loader to the
grave and filled it. After they had tamped down and
smoothed the dirt they each removed their hats again as
they shook hands with me. As I drove off, I understood
my vocation in new dimension. Though the political
will that it is our national obligation to care for the
least among us has faltered in the national debate of
the past generation, my sense that I was doing what my
commission demanded for Eva Mae, flooded my body.

Might those grave diggers have had some sense of
the holiness of their vocation? Could I have done more
to help them see their job as not only a job, but a sacred
duty? Should I have tipped them?

Waking the Life Force

Vocation wakes the life force waiting in us, urging us toward that place we are being "called" to spend our energy. The degree to which we can allow that calling to embrace us is the degree to which we dare let ourselves become fully alive. Engaged. Not merely going through the motions.

Inevitably, we often fudge; duck those moments—moments we can come to regret. We sometimes recognize them in retrospect. Our regret is a measure of how much of the road we have yet to travel. How much we depend on something—Someone—with the power to help us overcome our weakness.

It's not a moral issue, not should or ought. It's about just how alive we think we can manage. And then take a step beyond, into the unknown.

Embracing vocation, costs. The saying, "The truth shall set you free," tells the first half of the story. The second half: "Yes, but first it will set you back."

Affirming the dignity of everyone, regardless of station, first requires affirming my own integrity, my own worth, which turns out to be a life's work.

The essential worth of every person, every creature, rock, every inch of creation.

In *The Warmth of Other Suns,* by Isabel Wilkerson, a wise Black woman, part of the northern migration, says, "God don't make no mistakes."

Imagine! Everything we can see or conceive of: valuable. Sacred. Perfect. When they seem to go wrong it is almost always because we have tried to control (manage) what is calling us to risk going outside our comfort zone.

My experience of this conviction about self-worth began with an encounter that at first blush seems to be nearly its opposite.

Merciless, Merciful Doctor

Being born again can be a cliché in my trade, empty, meaningless. But not always. I take it to require dying, almost literally, before rebirth can happen.

Unscheduled Encounter — Dying to Self

I'd just had my 30th birthday. Still pretty new and uncomfortable, lost, in the priest role I'd stepped into. But too scared to seek the help of a therapist, afraid of what the therapist might uncover.

Under the guise of wanting professional advice, I began going to a member of the bishop's staff who I thought wise. And safe. Maybe my third visit—made up mostly of complaints about everyone and everything, in my life—seemingly out of the blue, he asked when I'd had my last physical.

I couldn't remember. "Time you did," he said. "I want you to go see this guy." He handed me a piece of paper with name and address.

Two weeks later I went.

I didn't see the doctor that day—I was run through a battery of tests, told to return two weeks later.

When I did, I was ushered into the office of this doctor I'd yet to meet. He was sitting behind his desk, shuffling through my test results. He hardly looked up at me, motioned to the chair in front of his desk, continued shuffling through the papers.

He muttered, *stage whisper*, "Jesus Christ, what a mess. Good lord."

He finally looked at me. His opening words: "A fat thirty-year old is an obscenity.

"Reading your test results I'm clear I wouldn't be your doctor for all the money in the universe. The way you're going, you won't make it to forty."

He paused to make sure I was still able to listen. Then: "You're twenty pounds overweight. When was the last time you did anything more strenuous than lifting a fork? How much do you drink?"

"I usually have a drink before dinner, sometimes two," I lied.

"Yeah, I'll bet. How much do you smoke?"

"Maybe a half a pack a day." Another lie.

"Really? You're a pretty good liar, too. Handy for a minister who probably doesn't believe in God. I bet you're in a lousy marriage, too."

I was so stunned I can't remember what happened after that, or how the encounter ended. I do remember sitting at the wheel of my car, so filled with anxiety I didn't dare turn on the ignition.

Fifty years later I understand that some significant piece of me died in that doctor's office. Wish I could tell you I was reborn on the spot, but it took several years of therapy, alcohol abstention, cold turkey from cigarettes, returning to the tennis court, learning to take long walks. Divorce, suicidal impulses, all had their innings with me before the person I hadn't known I longed to be, could hope to be born. The labor pains were long and hard.

No wonder it's called being born again.

When I told a colleague about seeing that doctor, he said, "Oh, so you went to see Dr. Adams. The diocese sends all the fucked-up clergy to see him. Didn't you hate him?"

Well, yes, at the time I did. Until pretty far down the road I recognized that he was Jesus for me that day. Midwife to my rebirth.

Somehow, I, like probably every sentient being, had sensed that embracing the life-energy given to me was not inevitable. Letting it see light required a new level of trust, attention, new behavior. What then to make of a moment like that doctor visit?

A seed. Tiny, like a mustard seed dropped into the earth, needs to split open before it can grow to full stature. (Jesus parable: Matthew 13)

That rude doctor made me see I was squandering my seed. By Grace alone the strident, seductive voice that had been shaping my life, striving to become more important, never completely drowned out that still, small, haunting voice calling me into life-giving, vulnerable intimacy with everyone and everything.

Had it not been that doctor, would there have been some other person, or crisis, that would crack open the self-defeating path I was on? Maybe. I can't quite believe there is a set path we're destined for. It may be that if we have a sense of what we hope our life might become, our unconscious energies may eventually help us find our way. But not without reverses we would probably avoid if we could.

Ironically, I see the fraught moment in that doctor's office as a moment of nearly unmanageable intimacy, openness, love, that dared me—demanded—that I own up to my failings, lacks. Begin to see another path. How to manage that revelation, acknowledging my limits, my lacks, my self-defeating habits, fear, without squashing the energy to keep going, is a learned, life-long discipline.

It never ceases needing renewing.

Even Conscientious Eating

For ten years I was a vegetarian, mostly because I didn't like animals being killed to sustain me. I ate vegetables. And eggs. Congratulated myself for taking a step closer to acknowledging the worth of every creature.

Whenever I fall into congratulating myself for doing something noble, there's a crash ahead.

I lost the thread of that dietary discipline in such a seemingly heroic way.

Our time in southern Africa was during their summer. Meat was one of the precious few sources of needed protein. As the local Padre I was sometimes guest of honor at banquets in the bush, ceremonially presented a slaughtered, barbecued antelope.

It would have been rude to refuse. I not only played the proper part, eating the offered meat, I loved it. My taste for meat returned. I have never returned to being vegetarian. Add that to the many ways I have fudged, shaved off the sharp edges of my vocation. I must have set myself on the vegetarian path a dozen times in the years since, only to have my will tested by a quarter pounder, and found wanting.

Still seeking the road back to being vegetarian. Would that bring me closer to ... ?

The Seduction of Flattery

I was rector of two parishes. Ancient ecclesiastical and cultural polity encouraged people to defer to me. I usually know when someone is using flattery, inviting my collusion, protecting the power our culture confers on people like us.

They sometimes refer to me as "doctor." There is such a thing as an honorary doctorate (unearned, usually given in return for a big donation), and even a Ph.D. in theology, neither of which I have.

Lists habitually put Dr. before the names of MDs. And clergy are listed as The Rev. Why doctor, priest, why not an honorific for Teacher, or Plumber?

Looking back I can see ways I have exploited the privileged position of clergy. It embarrasses me, yet even in old age, long retired, I continue to enjoy a few remaining pieces of it in ways I am reluctant to admit. You may have detected a few I haven't recognized.

Can I, given those caveats, still claim my vocation to make whatever small dents I can in the Domination System?

Maybe the issue is the reverse, calling on me to acknowledge the toxic effects the Domination System continues to make significant dents in how I spend my life.

Some of the most compelling moments in my life have come from finding energy to face down my prejudices enough to embrace people my history and conditioning tell me to consider lesser than me.

Like Gertrude who cared for me with such tenderness, and Booker, the African catechist who ushered me through moments of pastoring an African parish that I would have made a mess of on my own.

Designed for This?
Living a Parable

I sometimes remember the moment, early in my odyssey, I discovered God's sense of humor that helps me not take myself and my vocation too seriously.

On a bitter cold day, during Christmas break, senior year in college, I went for an interview at the now defunct Episcopal Theological School in Cambridge, Massachusetts. Rain the day before had coated the roads just before the temperature plummeted, forming a thin layer of ice everywhere.

As I stepped from my Nash Rambler (this was 1962), my feet went out from under me. I reached out with both hands to break my fall. The ice opened a small, bloody wound in each palm.

As I entered the Dean's office the secretary asked if I had an appointment.

I held out my hands, palms up, revealing my stigmata. "I'm here for an admissions interview," I said.

She looked startled, then laughed, and said, "No need for an interview, you're in."

Like many clergy I found ways to soften my discomfort about how cheeky it is to act as if I know the unknowable, ineffable God.

Every attempt to find new idioms, ways to reconsider ancient dogma, carried risks.

Ready for Prime Time?

Thirty-two-years-old, newly vetted rector of a parish in Dedham, a pre-revolutionary, Yankee, suburb of Boston, I decided the long-established, solemn, three-hour Good Friday Watch service, made up of Jesus' words from the cross, punctuated by hymns, silence, prayers, could use some livening up.

I found a troop of four young actors, who agreed to act out the drama of the crucifixion in our old, stone, Gothic church. Three men and a woman arrived draped in revealing togas. They gave a compelling, loud, frightening performance in which the woman (Mary Magdalene), on her knees, pulled herself the length of the aisle, moaning, slapping every other pew with an open palm creating an unnerving sound. I silently prayed she wouldn't slap old Mrs. McCleod's pew, which she, of course, did, nearly knocking the old lady's hat off. The Jesus actor, tied to the rood screen that separated the nave from the sanctuary, moaned, breathing heavily, noisily, and then, seemingly not at all.

The older, upper-class congregation who had come, expecting hymns and readings, sat in stoic silence through the ordeal.

When it was over I stood before the stunned people, stuttered something about how hard it had been to experience this, as I suggested it must have been to have been present for Jesus' crucifixion.

When everyone had left, I went to my office and called the Senior Warden, the head lay person, who had chaired the search that brought me there.

"I'm calling to offer my resignation," I said.

"Can you fill me in a little?" he asked.

I told him the story. His silence couldn't have been as long as it seemed.

"I don't suppose Jesus had such a great Good Friday either," he said. "I don't accept your resignation."

It's as if I am finding, everywhere, evidence that, sometimes wittingly, maybe more often unwittingly, I have been living a vocation—*a strong feeling of suitability for a particular career or occupation* (Collegiate Dictionary)—having to face down the foreboding it still arouses in me.

Would I have liked more clarity about having been chosen for that vocation?

I can still cringe at the ways I have fudged and shirked a role that so often seemed to require more weight than I thought I could carry.

How much do any of us, fully, consciously, choose our life path? How much is chosen for us by the ways we are shaped early, largely beneath consciousness?

By motions beyond reach of our intellect.

Maybe one measure of vocation is our natural resistance to it.

"Whoever finds his life will lose it, while the one who loses his life, for my sake, will find it." (Matthew 10).

Doesn't come across as an invitation one would jump at.

How offensive it would have been to devout Jews, for Jesus to use a despised Samaritan as the hero for one of his stories? How often vocation means choosing for what we might steer clear of.

I think we do understand, though powerfully conditioned by our culture, the ways we try to make ourselves successful—admired, climb the pyramid to power—lacks the power to satisfy our longing to live an authentic life.

The Last Shall Be First

A long out-of-print book I love: *Toting The Lead Row*, by Ruby Pickens Tartt, great-aunt of a friend. She was a folklorist in Alabama who, during the Depression, was commissioned to collect stories about poor rural Blacks. She recorded and reproduced them in local dialect. Remarkable for a White woman whose family were "The People," in that part of rural Alabama.

As I read those stories I was taken back to my childhood in North Carolina. I loved to sit on the kitchen counter, listening to the conversation of our Black maids and gardener as they traded stories and reflected on the soap operas they loved to listen to on the radio. I loved listening to them talk. They seemed to have hold of some way of being human together, kind of an easy intimacy I hadn't experienced in my own family. I also understood that, appealing as I found their humor and comradery, their colloquial language and accents, it wouldn't fly in the world for which I was being prepared.

The world I have inhabited ever since.

Gertrude, Hiawatha, Willy, began ordaining me for hearing Jesus in ways that didn't support our White, upper-class wish to be more important than poor, disenfranchised people like them. I don't suppose I had any idea of that at the time, but as I became immersed in the counter-cultural teaching of the Nazarene Rabbi, their voices resonated. Would they be surprised to know that?

Maybe not.

Believe In???

I don't *believe* in reincarnation, any more than I *believe* in God.

It wasn't the rational, *believing* part of me that chose to be ordained.

I am a creature of our culture, never tiring of trying to refine language that might shed light on the way my life has unfolded. My stubborn, linear, rational self, still very much intact and wishing to be in charge, occasionally catches a glimpse of that other dimension, beneath reason.

I was born in 1940, into what until recently was the unchallenged, dominating cohort in United States: White, male, affluent.

Some of the choices I made within the boundaries of that legacy, seem to suggest a longing to reconnect with an earlier legacy. Before my worldly ambitions gained such a strong foothold.

Deep in my heritage? Former life?

So, it's stories all the way. If unpacking how we became who we are seems too abstruse for our rational minds to unpack, telling our stories may take us a little closer.

I read a piece which says the role of father, as anything other than progenitor, is peculiar to our species, and few others. It pointed out that American fathers were largely absent from daily family life until very recently. The article says even busy, distant, fathers play a larger role than fathers of most other species.

This morning at a restaurant for breakfast, I watched a mother and father take delight in their months-old son, treating him with the respect I was taught was reserved for accomplished adults.

Mother Bear

I sometimes find myself wishing I might revisit my parenting days, immerse myself in the lives of my children. I often remember that painful lesson I learned from Lacey in what fierce parent love looks like.

That day, early in my marriage to Lacey when I took a carrot stick off her son's high-chair tray and he wailed, and Lacey laid me out in lavender, I learned a dimension of parent fierceness I hadn't tasted before.

I had three daughters from my first marriage, but this experience of the primordial role of parents, and the distinction between how father and mother may live them, was a discomforting revelation.

In liturgical churches—Roman Catholic, Anglican, Lutheran—clergy have long been called *Father* (since the latter two began ordaining women, they have begun referring to them as *Mother*).

The ecclesiastical role—modeled by Jesus, who history suggests never imagined he was forming a new church—*nurturing* father, appealed to me more than the *dominant* father I experienced growing up. The paradox—the seemingly unbridgeable gap between nurturer and rector, pastor and king—speaks to the enduring, medieval polity of the hierarchical Episcopal Church, a design more about domination than nurturing.

There's a growing sense that the church is finally inching towards embracing nurturing the wounds in everyone, even when it means surrendering some of the hierarchical power—but history and institutional survival instinct, run deep.

Liturgy as Good Drug

Tom Minifie, the complex, fun, colleague, and my associate for nine years in Dedham, was the most candid preacher I knew in revealing what mattered most to him about seeking God. His plain-spoken, unpolished preaching touched those who came prepared to be challenged. Others found him perplexing, even offensive.

Tom had done his share of experimenting with mind-altering drugs.

"If I come away from a sermon or worship without a good buzz, I feel like I was cheated. When you have an authentic encounter with the Holy Spirit it sets you to buzzing, like a good drug trip."

Having skipped the '60s drug scene, I only partially understood what Tom was talking about. At first, I considered it druggie propaganda.

As I began to understand Tom's point in saying worship invites us into an encounter with untutored parts of ourselves, I expanded my fairly surface meditation practice. If a God-encounter doesn't expand, enliven, confound our sense of reality, maybe it isn't an encounter with God. Maybe another illusion we harbor hoping we might satisfy our religious duty without having to change too much. Longing for God, but not too much God. Something in us knowing the fearsome, wondrous, loving, life-altering God will take us too far over, or out of our heads.

Tom became rector of a small parish in southern Ohio.

There a curious (to me) set of circumstances altered Tom's life-path and that of his wife, Jennifer, and their children.

Several months after Tom became rector of the Ohio parish Jennifer gave birth to Sylvia. She had Down's, with significant life-threatening anomalies. Tom and Jennifer were at first lost. How to cope with a child with such profound needs? Tom's parishioners, used to the rector supporting them in crisis, were paralyzed, unable to turn that dynamic the other direction.

Jennifer and Tom felt abandoned. Angry.

Then they connected with clergy and members of a local evangelical congregation. That group brought them food, organized a prayer group that met regularly to pray for Sylvia and her parents. When Sylvia needed to be hospitalized, that church arranged for people to spell Tom and Jennifer, taking up watch by Sylvia's bed.

The worship style of the supportive church was different from Episcopal worship. They raised their hands in the air to praise God, were "slain in the spirit," full-body embraced each other, spoke in tongues.

Rather than turn in fear from Tom and Jennifer's crisis, they rallied.

Tom told me he was drawn to their ways, initially because he was so grateful for their support. He found their love for God, for each other, palpable, not couched in ancient liturgical formulas. He said worship in the Episcopal Church left him stranded in his head. His heart untouched.

When he worshipped with his new friends he usually came away with a good "buzz."

I mentioned Tom's turn toward evangelical enthusiasm to John Coburn, Bishop of Massachusetts. John had known Tom's father, rector of a large parish in NYC. Both of us knew Tom's brother, then President of the College of Preachers in D.C. Everything in Tom's background spoke of Episcopal hierarchy. Bishop Coburn and I were surprised that Tom would embrace a tradition so contrary to his upbringing.

"He's a sensible boy," John, a hero and model for me, said. "He'll come around when this crisis subsides."

Tom never did "come around." After several years in which our friendship cooled because of his impatience with my safer path, we renewed our relationship.

Sylvia died before her second birthday, Jennifer, Tom and their new evangelical friends alongside her. After three more daughters, born and raised, Jennifer and Tom, two strong, independent people, chose separate lives. They didn't divorce, stayed in close touch, continuing to care for each other, but not as a together couple.

Tom retired from parish ministry, opened a small shop, selling collectibles, furniture, lamps, signs from the 1930s '40s, '50s. He loved it.

Tom called one day to tell me he'd been diagnosed with terminal cancer. He hoped palliative treatment might give him more good time.

I asked him if knowing he was going to die set up that buzz.

He laughed. "Getting louder," he said. "One day soon I expect it to drown out the distracting cacophony of this world."

I keep Tom's last voice message, August 2017, on my phone. He said the cancer had spread to his brain. Yet he was upbeat, poignant, present. Even funny. By the time I tried to call him again he had died.

What I'm still hoping to learn from Tom all these years since he died, is how to lower the barriers I'm conditioned to keep high to protect me from too close an encounter with the Holy Spirit.

Tom was laconic, not given to showing emotion. Somehow, he learned to let himself be embraced by God's fearsome love. He told me Sylvia had been his teacher.

He's not the first or only one I've known who learned new life-lessons from a person with Down's. Learned to see God revealed in someone the world wants to dismiss.

Our next-door neighbors had twin boys, one with Down's, the other not. We have watched with admiration as they have raised them, loving them. The boy with Down's, while fully functional physically, doesn't speak. The parents and his brother recognize his unique gifts and he is included in every family function. In my better moments I catch a glimpse of God shining through him more transparently than in most of us.

Unless you've lived with someone who is Down's it's easy to romanticize the open, fun, accepting, playfulness they can bring into our lives.

It's also frustrating, often enraging. They can disrupt the most carefully planned day. Make a mess of attempts to keep things tidy.

Might be an apt description of what it can be like to be visited by God's spirit.

Tom never tried to persuade me to follow him out of the staid old Episcopal scheme to the more emotional, open expression of God-encounter. I found his sweet reaching out to me, tolerant of my timid frustrations with being too timid to have a more immediate sense of God, moving. I think he, mercifully, accurately, thought I was too old, too "successful" at ascending church hierarchy to let go of all that.

More than two decades after retiring, gradually experiencing release from the responsibility to reassure parishioners that a brush with religion won't cause them to have to overturn their lives, I began to experience precisely that. Of having my own caution tempered by the wonder of life turning upside down as I age.

It's been a long time since I wore a clerical collar, stood in a pulpit an austere five feet above a congregation.

Though there are moments in which I miss the access granted to people in positions of authority, there is relief, even pleasure in feeling a greater sense of solidarity with what the Prayer Book refers to as "all sorts and conditions of people."

And I've discovered, as have a few of my colleague friends, that stepping down from those symbols of ecclesiastical hierarchy has opened paths to intimacy in new dimensions.

Death by Domination

A friend's son, a high school friend of our children, killed himself at age 48. Bright, funny, successful. Seems his career had crashed, along maybe with his marriage.

Like so many men I encountered in the parishes where I worked, he was shaped to take his place among the successful, dominant men he saw around him. Like all of us he had his ups and downs. Maybe, during his most recent down, he despaired of ever claiming what he felt was his birthright. His mandate.

His parents asked me to officiate at the burial of his ashes. To my distress, and yet oddly welcome, the decades since I felt responsible for spreading balm on people's distress has diminished the distance I have so carefully kept to protect myself from being swept up by my own grief. I came unglued burying that young man. I'm sure his family saw that I barely managed the prayers through my sobbing.

Not only because I had known him since he was a boy, and liked him, but because I projected my own life experience onto his suicide, despair, his fear he'd been defeated in the struggle to fill the "successful," dominant, male expectation.

Retiring from ordained life while I still had energy for new exploration has excused me from having to inhabit that role. Yet it's still lodged in my bones. Takes very little to wake it. The possibility that the young man despaired of fulfilling what he felt was expected of him, what he expected of himself, woke up all those old anxieties in me.

Go in peace dear man, and may the peace of God, which passes all understanding, be yours.

Ghost Encounters

Since I first began tending people's dying and death, I have sometimes experienced an odd, unsettling sensation. On my way to visit their bodies, bury them, I sense an awkward, indistinct presence traveling with me.

Sometimes it's as if someone opened a window on a cool, breezy day.

I mentioned this to a friend, steeped in the Zen tradition.

"That's the person who has died," she explained. "Sometimes they haven't completed their journey into the next world. And they're not sure what they're experiencing, why people they love are bereft. They sense you may be open to recognizing, acknowledging them.

"Talk to them. Explain they have died. Those of us who love them are having a hard time letting them go. Reassure them that we'll be all right. We need to go through this hard, painful part, confusion, grief, before our new, unfamiliar relationship across the boundaries of mortality, can begin to evolve. Tell them it's OK for them to leave when they're ready."

To western rational thinking, it sounds spooky, even a little nuts.

Try it the next time someone you love dies. Not only may you discover your connection to a new dimension of reality, your love not dead, but evolving into a powerful new love. It makes room for your grief to include gratitude. For love that doesn't die when we do, a taste of eternity.

Thank you, Tom. Thank you, Sylvia.

•

Along with a handful of other predictable features of old age, I have been visited with sleep issues. Some nights I lie awake all night.

Along about 3 A.M., I begin to panic.

What's going to happen to me if I don't sleep?

In the Bible passage in 1 Samuel, the boy Samuel is wakened in the night by a voice calling to him. Thinking it is his mentor, Eli, paging, three times he gets up and goes to Eli, asking what he wants.

The third time, Eli, says, "Go back, lie still, and when the voice calls again, say, 'Here am I, Lord.'"

Samuel did as Eli told him. God comes and says, "I am about to do something that will make the ears of all who hear, tingle."

When you read what God's voice was saying to Samuel, you understand why we ignore that voice. That tingle is initially fear. Seldom what we expect or hope to hear.

God was telling Samuel that Eli, Samuel's mentor, was going to come under severe judgment for his stiff-neckedness. Samuel was being commissioned to call out the most important man in his life, the leader of the Hebrews. As if that weren't enough, God was preparing Samuel to take over Eli's role.

What kind of chutzpah is required to tell your mentor he's to step aside to make room for you?

Discerning God calling makes your ears tingle with excitement. And fear.

Excitement for being chosen for a role we hadn't imagined.

Fear, because it's calling us to venture out of where we think we want to be, need to be, must be, to someplace we know is beyond our powers. Maybe it's not God, but my imagination, fantasy. Turns out to be where we all live, struggling to shape reality for ourselves, reality we hope we can manage even while hunger for more.

Something in us knows we're designed for that more, feel unfinished until and unless something sweeps us out of our comfort zone, into an unmanageable, uncomfortable unknown where our vocation waits.

Lucky for Samuel, Eli knew who had spoken to Samuel. He understood there was nothing he could or should do to try to alter what was coming.

Samuel would replace Eli.

Imagine Joe Biden telling Donald Trump that God had told him that he, Biden, was going to replace

Trump. Maybe God had already told Trump, which could explain his manic, destructive behavior.

Guess God's speaking didn't end with the biblical prophets?

I usually forget my dreams. Or think I do. Last night I had at least two dreams that felt of consequence.

In the first, a woman I can't identify seduced me. But it wasn't the erotic sort of dream it might once have been. I was aware that I was on top of her, but our bodies weren't merging. The sexual excitement I would have expected was absent. Soon I realized she was gone. I went looking for her. She was walking rapidly away.

"You seem to want to get away from me," I said.

"Maybe that's because I am," she answered.

In the other dream I was trying to find my way somewhere. What was unsettling was it was someplace familiar. Unable to work out the way there made me panic. Eventually I found myself in a room filled with familiar people. One, a high school classmate who died last year. He reassured me that I would eventually find my way, and warned me that it was going to become increasingly difficult to find an easy route to places I needed to go.

When I woke I thought about those dreams. From the first I discerned that my lifelong habit of making my way by charming, "seducing" people, long ago ran its course. Another not-very-subtle prompt, to forsake my the façade that had seemed to win me easy intimacy. There is no such thing.

In the second dream I took my dead classmates'

counsel to mean that in this late chapter I am on a journey with landmarks that seem familiar, they are in fact leading me someplace entirely new. He reassured me that I will get there, but not by navigating in the old ways. And not without many uncharted hazards.

Rich dreams.

And there's daydreaming, whatever we mean by that. Becoming aware of non-linear sequence filtering into misty consciousness.

Old School Ties Unravel

We're having dinner tonight with friends. Why did my focus turn to his having gone to St. Mark's School as a boy? Which led to my thinking about having gone to a rival school. And to my time years later as a singularly ineffective trustee of my old school with which I have an uneasy, increasingly distant relationship?

An experience I had with the school and my niece helped me come to terms with my ambivalence toward what that school reveals to my identity.

My sister was in destructive conflict with her early teen daughter. She wondered if I might influence my old boarding school to admit her daughter.

I told her I was sure I could arrange an interview.

I knew my niece just well enough to suspect my old New England boarding school was just what she didn't need and wouldn't want.

I drove the two of them to the school. She had an interview with John Quincy Adams Doolittle, Director of Admissions. I doubt she was aware of the significance of that freighted name, but I suspected, whether she was or not, the stuffy atmosphere of the school would put her off.

Before we left, Jay Doolittle took me aside. "Are you aware of the home situation?" he asked. I said I knew things were tense, but not much more.

"I asked her why she wanted to go to boarding school," he said. "You know what she said? She said she was afraid if she stayed home she might kill her mother."

I knew my niece just well enough to know how much she liked to shock people, especially those she thought stiff and proper. I also suspected she wanted to make certain they wouldn't admit her. Which they didn't.

Not long after, the decision was made that she would go live with her father. Her relationship with her mother, my sister, remained distant until her mother was dying. They reconciled days before her mother died. I watched that renewing of their relationship with overflowing emotion, strengthening the promise that it's never too late to dare to love.

My sister's remaining open to the possibility of reconciling with her daughter helped me savor the same thing with my sister.

She was an aging hippie. A bearer of unconventional, love as nearly unconditional as we humans seem able to sustain. Just days before she died I finally understood that her off-beat life wasn't driven by mere contrariness, but by brave dissension from a commercial culture she found stultifying, spirit-killing.

She visited me in a dream recently in which I understood her to say, "It's OK, Blayney, everything's going to be all right. So get on with it." Thank you, Sylvia.

A friend my age said, "Now when I wake up, I say to myself, 'One day closer to your death; so what do you want to do with this day?'"

All that, triggered by an upcoming dinner with friends?

Yep. It's always right there, beckoning.

Fascinating, enlightening, watching your consciousness travel a labyrinth. Doesn't seem far-fetched that the cells that came together to form you—beginning with an unlikely sperm and egg—cells that must have once been a part of other beings, might float unbidden into your consciousness.

Is This All There Is?

Your skin regenerates every 27 days. Cells lining your stomach every couple of days. Red blood cells about 4 months. White cells 10 years. Bones regenerate every 10 years.

The Law of Conservation of Energy says that the energy that you are, have, spend, is never lost. Is that immortality?

Of a sort. Alas, it doesn't support our dreams of living forever in a form that is familiar. It says your energy somehow survives. But the Second Law of Thermodynamics says that over time energy, in every system (person), becomes more disorganized, dispersed. Eventually it no longer can sustain the complex system it once ran. What we call death must be the scattering of the unique organization of cells, the integrity we identify as us.

Where do those cells go? God knows. But does it seem far-fetched to wonder, in moments of strong openness, unusual receptivity, that cells that organized the sacred, complex energy I knew as my big sister, might make its way into my deep conscious? The love that joined us seeking a new path?

I'm not so much suggesting a new understanding of death as I am entertaining the possibility, maybe certainty, that the ether in which we float has more dimensions than causality can calculate.

I'm hardly the first to find exploring our mortality rich, thrilling. Some consider me obsessed. I accidentally typed those two previous sentences twice, hitting a bunch of wrong keys. Yes, I'm a clumsy typist, but I suspect those errors were more from anxiety in revealing my timid venturing into territory I don't understand. Or even "know" exists.

Deliberate Death

In addition to suicides of parishioners and friends, I have known a handful of people who have chosen medical—in those days unlawful—deliberate deaths.

The bravest was a mother who's 16-year-old son had aggressive, metastatic cancer that was eating away his abdomen, causing him intractable pain.

A year after diagnosis, having undergone endless debilitating treatment, he was confined to bed, unable to take nourishment, requiring more and more pain killer.

I came by to see him on a Friday afternoon. His doctor was there. As the doctor, the boy's mother, and I stood by the bedside, the doctor laid out several syringes of morphine.

"I'm going to be away for the weekend," the doctor said. "You can always call one of my colleagues. But I think I've left you enough morphine to get you through until Monday."

He picked up the first syringe. "This should be enough for managing most of his pain. But if it doesn't you can give him the second dose. If that doesn't stop the pain, I'm sure a third shot will. But I can't be sure if that might cause him to go into respiratory failure. Die."

The mother nodded that she understood. I thought I did too.

Sunday afternoon she called me. "He's gone."

I went right over. We stood by her son's bed. "He's finally out of pain," she said. "He looks so peaceful. It's the first time in weeks I haven't had to watch him squirm, trying to find a position that would lessen the pain."

I noticed the syringes had all been used.

I hugged her. "You're the bravest, most wonderful mother I can ever imagine. He was so lucky to have you for a mother."

We both wept.

"I was desperate, not brave," she said. "I tried so hard to help him. I hope I did the right thing."

"The doctor, and God, took a while to catch up to you in caring for him," I said. When I came into this room and saw you standing by the bed, I understood Michelangelo's *Pieta* in a whole new way."

•

Angela had been a part of the Blessed Group, those with terminal diagnosis, who met in my office weekly. She'd lived with cancer for many years, enduring one tough treatment after another. Somehow her sense of humor got her through the pain and indignity. She had to endure regular colonoscopies which she called "the big up-yours."

She was bed-ridden when I came for one of my last visits. She told me she had read *Final Exit; The Practicalities of Self-Deliverance*, by Derek Humphry, that sets out a step-by-step recipe for ending one's life painlessly.

"I'm ready," Angela said. Her son and daughter, both in their late 40s, had agreed to sit with her while she took pills mixed into ice cream and drank a large glass of vodka. "If you want to be there, too, that would be just fine."

I wish I had taken her up on that. At the time it felt too radical, too much as if I would be taking a more active role in ending her life than I was ready for. I told her I loved her, admired her courage, and faith. I laid hands on her head, committed her to God.

"I understand," she said. "You've been wonderful through all this. I'm so grateful. I'll ask the kids to call you when I stop breathing. Then you can come pray over my body and provide them solace."

It all happened just as she intended. In looking back over more than 20 years to that time, I hope today I would be there with her children.

What changed?

I'm no pathfinder. Death is no longer a forbidden subject. At 81, it seems almost welcome, hardly as ominous as it once was.

I don't congratulate myself about this. I suspect just about all of us would look full-on into what to make of knowing we'll die if it didn't make us feel too weird.

•

The son of friends, who went to school with a couple of our children, died of an overdose. Fentanyl got mixed in with his usual dose of heroin.

When I called to express my sadness, his mother said she thought he overdosed by accident. She said he had long been addicted to heroin and had managed, as some can, to continue to lead a useful if less demanding, life. He'd come to live with his parents the year before he died. He told them there was "bad stuff" out there that he meant to stay clear of. He told them if he ever accidentally got a bad dose, with Fentanyl, it would likely kill him. She told me the year he'd been at home it had been wonderful.

"He was a model son to his aging parents. Always looking for ways to help us, so cheerful. Endlessly good company."

It's a story I once couldn't have imagined. Uncomfortably common now.

Sad as it is, I take it as a tentative step toward embracing death as part of life. In some perverse way that young man and his mother, having struggled for years to find a different path, had come to terms with life—and death—as it clearly was for them. He was addicted, owned up to that. His parents had stopped trying to be his drug gate-keepers, accepting his reality.

Treating him as the integrity-filled, whole person they loved. He'd found ways to maintain his habit that didn't require the anti-social pathologies we associate with addiction.

No longer shameful pathology, no more sneaking around.

Tough Choices

Deliberate death can divide families.

Katherine, 92-year-old widow, matriarch of one of the most prominent clans in the community, was diagnosed with terminal cancer. She told me she had a wonderful life and was ready for it to be over.

She also told me her family wanted no part of talking with her about it, insisted on continually reassuring her that she would be cured. She, too, read *Final Exit* and followed it to the letter. Including wrapping her head in a plastic bag after she'd taken all the things required, to make certain when she lost consciousness she would asphyxiate and die.

After she died, her nephew, a fellow Episcopal priest, asked me to preach the homily at her service. "I know you believe God's love overpowers everything," he said. "I can't stop believing that there are some things will land us in hell. And I think I'd have to say that Katherine's decision to play God with her own life might be a barrier to her salvation. I'd hate to have to say that at her service."

I admired his candor, his generous spirit in asking me to preach about Katherine's courage and God's all-powerful love that now embraces her more fully than ever.

I loved being able to stand before a congregation of her friends, family, admirers, assuring them that God's love for her, written all over her long, useful life, wasn't dented by her decision to embrace her dying. And that whatever the circumstances, love will see us through our own dying.

Systemic ~~Embedded~~ Racism: Our National Shame

Racism occupies a place similar to death in our national consciousness. It flies in the face of what we brag about, what we want to believe about ourselves. So, we obfuscate, deny.

The innate strength of the American experiment—inviting all sorts and conditions (except indigenous people), from all over the world is also fraught with problems.

Europeans came because they believed they had a better chance here to improve their lot.

And because they believed our sales pitch about democracy in which every voice counts.

Though Irish and Italian immigrants found the road to success rockier than advertised, their odyssey, like those who came before, they often found hard work and perseverance was a passport to a good life for many.

Africans, darker skinned, brought, not by their dreams, but in chains, more than two centuries later still struggle for justice, equal access.

As upper-class, White, my people here for several generations, I believe passionately in civil and equal rights, have worked and demonstrated for justice.

But...

Racism. Troubling, not only because it's so persistent, so pervasive, but because, despite what I believe, African-American Americans still seem somehow "other" to me.

When I mentioned racism in preaching I was sometimes accused of being political instead of "spiritual."

I considered spiritual as having political consequences. "I will," we respond in the baptism service when we're asked if we promise to respect the dignity of every human being. That's *every* human being, White, Brown, Black. Poor, rich, *every* human being. If the first responsibility of government is, as basic political science claims, protection of its people, anything that diminishes people's well-being, resources weighted in favor of a small group, unequal access to full participation in decision-making, hearkens back to Jesus saying, "Inasmuch as you failed to reach out to one of the least of these, you turned your back on me."

How often must we say that our freedom, our well-being, is only as secure as the freedom and well-being of the least among us, before we grasp the reality that what we all long for, demands justice for everyone?

Bryan Stevenson, author of *Just Mercy*, creator of the Lynching Museum, cuts to the heart of it: "The opposite of poverty isn't wealth. The opposite of poverty is justice."

Late Life Reflection

If you live as long as I have you may reach a place at which your self-recriminations about lacks and offenses, failures and disappointments are cast in a new light. Instead of accusations against yourself they can be seen as limits that your personality and life circumstances seemed to impose.

Owning up to them, ceasing rationalizing, you may even experience those lacks and offenses losing some of their power to define and control you.

Daughter Carson opened a way for me to do that in a systematic way.

She subscribed me to *StoryWorth* which invited me, every week for the year 2021, to respond to some question.

A recent one may be the best way I am able to explain—especially to myself—the hard issue of race in my experience. The question:

What people of color had a significant impact on your life growing up? And in general?

My response, powerfully shaped by experience I've mentioned earlier:

> People of color have had a significant impact on my life, growing up and into the present day.
>
> Raised in the segregated south, we had Black maids, Black gardener, virtually all menial work done by Black people. Although it was never made explicit, I think I assumed they did that kind of work, lived in terrible housing, because they were inferior to White people, not capable of living and working in a more sophisticated environment. Our family doctor, perhaps the most revered person in our lives, told my father it was a scientific fact that Black people had thicker skulls, and therefore smaller brains. Looking back, I suspect my mother didn't believe that, mostly because she seemed to consider Gertrude, our cook/maid, smart, resourceful, a partner. But Mom wasn't brave about expressing unconventional views. I think I may have picked up both sides of that from her, because I still consider Gertrude maybe the earliest nurturing person in my life. But I doubt I would have dared say that out loud in those days.
>
> When we moved to the Philippines we had the usual colonial array of Filipino help. Maybe

hoping to make amends in some way for the demeaning way Gertrude had been treated, Mom bonded fiercely with Melie, our cook. It ended in disaster when Ambrosio, our driver, who I suspect was angry at the special treatment Melie received compared to the other servants, took my father out to the car one day, opened the trunk, and showed him things Melie had stolen from us, and demanded that he drive them to her house. It was a huge blow to our family because we had maintained the fiction that Melie had been treated as a virtual family member. Did we learn anything about the reality of unequal power relationships? I doubt it.

I went to small private boarding schools that in the 1950s were just beginning to experiment with admitting Black students. Cautiously, one at a time. If the tiny cohort was not already part of the establishment—maybe from one of the inner-city programs that identified promising students and provided money for elite education—the intent was clearly to shape them for the world the rest of us came from. We have learned in recent years, as many of those students of color have created web sites about their boarding school experience—that it was fraught with horrors.

The summer between my second and third year in seminary I taught at St. George's (Newport, RI) summer school. One of my assignments was to help prepare Conrad, a foster child from the local community, to begin St. George's the following fall. Conrad had never been off Aquidneck Island. He and I would sit over the *NY Times* each morning and read about something happening in Washington or Rome. He tried to look interested. It is a long, convoluted story, that ended two summers later when Conrad's foster mother scolded him about not being sufficiently grateful for all those kind White people at the school were doing for him. Conrad must have been harboring simmering anger for those two years. He hit his foster mother in the back of her head, thought he'd killed her, set the house on fire and fled. She was impaired, but survived. Conrad was arrested. In prison he hung himself. Hays Rockwell, school chaplain, who had been Conrad's champion, and I, among many others, had nowhere to put this horror. It was an early lesson for me in why noblesse oblige is cruel and thoughtless.

I was caught up in civil rights after that, a follower of Dr. King, John Lewis (who was exactly my age). Ed Rodman, a class behind me in seminary, was the first Black person I encountered who didn't hold back in expressing his anger at injustice, nor his contempt for do-good, White people like me who thought we could indemnify ourselves with right-thinking that didn't require making changes in our lives. Ed went on to become a major player in the struggle for justice in the Episcopal Church.

My daily life, in Jacksonville, Vermont, in the gentle months, La Jolla, California, in the winter, is in many ways as segregated as my growing up in Charlotte. The impact that Black Lives Matter has on me is to reinforce my sense, not only of the systemic racism embedded in me, but in the bones of our nation. Maybe people of color, Brown, Black, will continue to grow as a percentage of our population, and I hope will be able to exercise the power of their numbers that change requires.

I would love to believe that the fierce resistance to this justice that has come to dominate the Republican Party is the final dying energy of our country's slavery legacy. I won't live to see it, but I pray (and even sometimes work) for strengthening access of people who have been denied it, to the ballot, to education, work opportunity. Not only because I think it is just, but because unless it succeeds, our nation will join others in which power is controlled by an increasingly violent minority.

While racism remains in my bones—I'm still surprised, happily, to encounter a person of color as a peer—people of color have had as big an impact on my understanding of justice, as any group in my life.

•

Just yesterday—May 2021—walking in La Jolla, California, I noticed an Hispanic-appearing woman pull her Mercedes to the curb and get out. I found myself wondering if she was a rich Mexican or perhaps was driving the car for a family she works for.

So much simpler to let the deeply etched channels in my conscious run free. My prejudices rise, unexpectedly, uncomfortably, to the surface.

It's weird to be this age. I guess I expected to have excised this non-rational prejudice from my senses by now.

I can still ride a bike up some pretty demanding hills, albeit more slowly and in the lowly granny-gear. Hit tennis balls reasonably well for an hour and a half, albeit with less pace.

But emptying the washing machine I inevitably hit my hand on the edge of the opening and either cause an open bleed—wrecking the clean wash—or cause bruises that look as if I have been in a fight.

That's sort of what it's like now, eager to stay in the game, as well and as long as possible, while learning to accept increasing fragility, weaker muscles, less efficient lungs. Embarrassing weakening of short-term memory.

And to acknowledge embarrassing shortcomings, prejudices, without beating myself up.

That's a lesson I've spent this lifetime trying to learn: how to be honest and realistic about myself—especially the lacks—without turning that self-honesty into self-hate.

A journalist I have some contact with, wise, disgruntled, wrote that Billy Graham (the most unlikely person for him to speak with, maybe interviewing him?) counseled him to never think badly of himself. Good to acknowledge your lacks, things you hope to improve, but never to consider those lacks reason to deny you are created from love that cannot be revoked. Billy promised him that if he followed that he would have a happy life.

Ought to give it a try.

The pandemic has given octogenarians a chance to put our money where our mouths have been. One need only read the actuarial tables to understand, no matter how healthy we may be, the vast majority of life is behind us.

Like most people who trust the science, I was vaccinated and boosted as soon as I was eligible.

I'd like to live as long and as well as I can.

What to make of the gift of the remaining time?

Old Age Therapy

Friends my age speak of their "bucket list", places to see, books to read, tasks to accomplish while still relatively intact.

I've never had a bucket list. When I was laboring in the ecclesiastical vineyard, I dreamed of publishing a novel. I've published 5. I'm happy to have done that, but it was rather like winning a tennis tournament (hasn't happened in many a moon). Once done, those things take their place alongside most of what I have managed to accomplish in my life. Friends talk about things in their lives they would like to be able to do over.

I have perhaps overidentified with recent losses by Naomi Osaka and Novak Djokovic, tennis luminaries, both heavy favorites to win whenever they play.

Osaka, in her post-match interview said the game had become a nightmare for her. When she wins all she feels is relief. When she loses she feels awful, as if she'd failed her team, her supporters, and maybe worst of all, her own sense of owing the world and herself, success rather than failure.

This from the number one player in the world, who last year commanded more endorsement dollars than any other athlete.

It's vexing to feel you must measure up to whatever you perceive (or imagine) the world expects of you. Since it's not necessarily your own motivation that is providing energy for that, it's unlikely to provide satisfaction.

Maybe having survived, often thrived, through periods when I wondered if my choices, and events I didn't see coming, were going to bring me down, I am grateful to be able to look back and see how surprisingly well things have worked out. More often than not, despite, rather than because of, my own wiles.

Osaka and Djokovic have woken up issues in me I love to think I have managed to keep the world (and myself) from seeing. A fool's errand. At age 81 I entered into a new round of therapy, first time in many a moon.

Unlike earlier therapy in which I was trying to manage my fears and doubts so I could succeed, maybe even excel, rather than fail, now it's more about learning from and honoring my fears, anxiety, passions, motivations so I might spend my remaining energies acknowledging, even honoring them.

Introducing myself to myself, light and shadow, learning to trust what I discover, is not about strengths and weaknesses, good and bad, but about the person I am. Have longed to allow myself to be.

Though therapy is the discipline I choose for this, it feels like a religious quest. If God—Love—is the author of our being, then that's what we're made of, love, what we're made for. And can afford to embrace the whole package. What we're proud of, and what we find hard to own up to about ourselves.

I've long known there's more to this package than I can make sense of. Or had the courage to take a full-faced look at.

I've loved being a priest. Loved being married. A parent. Step-parent.

I've loved being alive. Human.

Each of them has had its surprises, asking more of me than I had native ability to meet. That's why I'm hooked on the notion of God's grace. Of the wonders I've experienced, so often coming as mysterious gifts, rather than my having won or earned them.

I began this odyssey with my fascination with death. The mystery that can make life richer and more fascinating, or terrifying, by its relentless reality.

What to make of it? How will it find me? When?

At this moment I see it as the capping off of a great adventure. Yet I reserve the right to be terrified.

Exciting adventure, terrifying abyss, God, love, will see me through.

I Hope When It Happens

BY DIANE SEUSS

I hope when it happens I have time to say oh so this is how
it is happening

unlike Frank hit by a jeep on Fire Island but not like dad
who knew too

long six goddamn years in a young man's life so long it
made a sweet guy sarcastic

I want time to say oh so this is how I'll go and smirk at that
last rhyme

I rhymed at times because I wanted to make something
pretty especially for Mikel

who liked pretty things soft and small things who cried into
a white towel when I hurt

myself when it happens I don't want to be afraid I want to
be curious was Mikel curious

I'm afraid by then he was only sad he had no money left was living on green oranges

had kissed all his friends goodbye I kissed lips that kissed Frank's lips though not

for me a willing kiss I willingly kissed lips that kissed Howard's deathbed lips

I happily kissed lips that kissed lips that kissed Basquiat's lips I know a man who said

he kissed lips that kissed lips that kissed Whitman's

lips who will say of me I kissed her who will say of me I kissed someone who kissed

her or kissed someone who kissed someone who kissed someone who kissed her

Whose lips might I kiss, and whose might they have kissed, and will I be happy, sad, scared, aware, or unaware?

Probably.

Acknowledgments

It would take another book twice this size to acknowledge the people who have nurtured and helped me through this long life. Beginning with my parents who died before I was gracious enough to be grateful, not only for their setting aside much of their own life for me, but giving me a shot at abundant life. In the book you encounter a panoply of those without whom my time here would have been poorer.

This memoir would have remained a vague memory were it not for a few who encouraged and nursed me through my uneasiness that it was nothing more than an exercise in narcissism.

My sister Perry Colmore, who, among her many amazing chapters, served as a newspaper editor for many years, and was the initial reader. She gave me heart even while finding the endless typos and grammatical disasters that mark my writing.

Castle Freeman, friend and fiction writer who has captured the unique idiom of Vermont voice, generously agreed to read the manuscript and provided invaluable help in ferreting out stories of little interest to anyone except me.

Dede Cummings, founder of Green Writers Press, has provided the expertise that totally mystifies me about the publishing world. This is the second book she has seen me through, and I promised her that if she would stick with me this time I would hang up my keyboard for good.

Lacey, who regards my writing as a distraction from daily chores, has nonetheless stuck with me and encouraged me for lo these forty-three years we have been married. It's more than I could have dared hope for. I owe her more than I know how to pay. Aside from mysticism, marriage is the most opaque, inscrutable institution humans have ever thought up. Lacey will never know how much she has impacted the ways I see the world. I doubt I am eloquent or generous enough to ever find ways to thank her adequately.

Heather, Jen, Carson, Louise, Oakley, children and step-children, who have marked my life and writing more than they could imagine.

So, near as it must be, the end hasn't shown up yet. Thanks to you for hanging with me a little longer. It only gets more interesting.

This book comes out on the eve of Thanksgiving, 2022. So many to thank for so much.